The Boy Who Wrote My Story

AF664157

Evincepub Publishing

Evincepub Publishing

Nehru Nagar, Bilaspur, Chhattisgarh 495001

First Published by Evincepub Publishing 2021

ISBN: 978-93-5446-184-2

THE BOY *who* WROTE MY STORY

By

NIHARA HAREESH

About The Author

Nihara Hareesh is many things- a lifestyle blogger, A TEDx speaker, an entrepreneur, a singer, film-maker and an avid traveler.

Originally from Kerala, India, she currently resides in Dubai. She graduated from Amity University Haryana in journalism and from New York Film Academy in Hi-Def Filmmaking.

She started her own lifestyle website 'Lifestyle Glossary' back in 2015 and co-founded her Dubai based media agency "Hyperlinks Media" with her partner in 2016. Since then she has worked with over 400 brands and spends most of her time writing and documenting her wanderlust conquests.She began writing at the age of 11. She had won multiple prizes for her poetry and short stories. Her first short story was published in 2008 called 'We Always Hurt the Ones We Love' in Gokulam magazine India.

Her first cover story about the safety of women in India was published in 'The Hindu' New Delhi edition back in June 2014.

'Relentless' is her debut book. "The Boy Who Wrote My Story" is her fourth book.

Nihara is also a TEDx speaker who recently delivered a speech on 'Power In Vulnerability' in Dubai.

Dedicated To

Rachit - The Boy Who Wrote My Story in real life.
Thank you for changing the narrative for the better.
Much Love

Contents

CHAPTER 1

"Hey, everyone. My name is Kiara, Kiara Sen."

As I struggled to look at the group of unfamiliar faces, their voices spoke back to me in unison,

"Hello, Kiara!"

My eyes ran across the well-lit yet forlorn four-walled space. The walls spoke colors of blue, and the air smelt of fresh coffee and stale cookies. I pondered over the words to say when a voice broke out from the corner of the room,

"Miss Sen! Would you like to start by telling us why you are here?"

Miss Rose's eyes met mine with an empathetic gaze. She was a soft woman in her mid-forties who strongly believed in seasonal change and the power of the universe - two things I strongly disbelieved in. Maybe that is what made her an exceptional counselor at the center. She sat a few inches away from me in a three-leg single chair holding a printed paper that contained the agenda of the day. Maybe it was her calming voice or a reassuring smile, but it gave me fortitude.

"I-I was an alcoholic and 18 months sober now. It's my last day here today, and I-I am glad," I stammered while I addressed all the unacquainted. They stared back at me with hope in their eyes. Hope for themselves. It was their first day at the center, and it was a tradition here for the success stories to welcome the dispirited with words of encouragement.

But If I could only put those words to paper! I thought to myself.

"We love your books! Are you planning to write another one soon?" a young girl in her early twenties questioned from the crowd,

"Perhaps about your time here?"

"I am glad you love my books but uh…. I don't think I will be writing anytime soon." I said, looking down to avoid any more questions. I could slowly feel a familiar uneasy emotion rise from the pit of my stomach. Is it too late to make a run for it? Would it be too rude if I excused myself? Is this what I have to deal with once I am out of here? The same perennial questions?

Thankfully Miss Rose noticed my discomposed state and decided to relieve me of my despair.

"Thank you, Miss Sen. We are glad to be a part of your recovery. We hope we never see you here again."

The whole room burst into a giggle. Miss Rose sure did know how to change the mood of the atmosphere with her quick wit. A quality I always admired. She had made it her mission to teach me the lightness of life during my time here. Did she succeed? I am not quite sure. But one thing is irrefutable. I am not the same Kiara who walked in here a year and a half back.

"Child! This life has so much to give you. Waste it not by choosing a temporary alternative. Remember the faces of those who love you and wish you well. Whenever you feel something, embrace it wholly - the pain and happiness. And remember to move on and always choose Love and Happiness."

She would recite these lines every time she spotted me pondering over a blank paper with my pen, under the only oak tree in the beautiful lush green garden the center had.

Happiness!

As a 26-year-old writer living in the most bustling and happening city of New Delhi in India, I had the luxury of associating happiness with fame, friends, and alcohol. But never love!

Love and happiness were two words I was never lucky enough to put together in one sentence. So I never understood it when Miss Rose casually dropped those words together like it was no big deal.

"Were you happy with your late husband? Did you love him, and did he love you back enough? How did it feel?" I asked her one day during our regular counseling sessions. Miss Rose was a widow who lost her husband to a battle with lung cancer seven years ago. She once recounted it as a reason for why she joined the center - to help people overcome their addictions. Perhaps, a way to compensate for the fact that her husband was an alcoholic with a smoking addiction, as well. Or to save a family from going through what she had.

"Was I happy with Vincent? Yes. The happiest.

Did I love him? Yes. I still do with my whole heart.

How did it feel? Like being saved from drowning in the ocean.

One cannot explain how love feels. It is different for different people. For me, it always felt like being saved from drowning in the endless vast ocean.

Did he love me back enough? Love is never enough. It is like asking if you have inhaled enough air to continue breathing for the rest of your life. It is never enough."

Her voice cracked as she completed the sentence. I should not have asked her that question, but her response stayed with me for a very long time. Her take on Love and Life was peculiar and something I have never heard of before.

Today was my last day at the Rehabilitation Centre.

“Have you got everything?” asked Miss Rose as she checked the discharge sheet. I had gathered all my belongings and was waiting at the reception to give her a final goodbye.

“Yes!” I said feebly and hugged her for the last time. “Thank You! You have been like a mother to me over the past few months, and I cannot thank you enough. It would not have been entirely possible without you.”

“Oh, Child! I am going to miss you. Take care of yourself.”, she said as she gave a small well-wrapped package in my hand, “For a rainy day! When you need some reminder about how far you have come. Do not open it till then.” I knew for sure it was the pile of encouragement letters from the staff they usually give out when one leaves the institution.

I smiled back at her kind gesture, slowly grabbed my suitcases, and headed out to the front door. As I made my way out of the rehabilitation center to the car, I stopped to look back at it one last time. Nostalgia hit me hard. I never liked the place, but I found solitude here. Something I might never get in the real world.

CHAPTER 2

"Surprise!"

I opened the door to my spacious two-bedroom apartment in Malviya Nagar overlooking the busy highway to spend a quiet evening all by myself. But alas! I found myself greeted by a room full of people I have not met in the past year. Confetti, cakes, and glasses filled with cider were all over the place. My casual denim jeans and tee shouted exhaustion in a field of partywear, but no one seemed to notice. Not the evening I had planned for months. Just light reading and warm milk would have sufficed.

Suddenly a woman in her mid-twenties wearing a sundress with clean-cut bangs covering her pretty face, and a familiar smile appeared before me and pulled me into her warm embrace. Rina was my best friend since we were schoolmates. We practically grew up together and have been each other's rock for as long as I could remember. The warm hug bought back a sense of solace, and I reciprocated with an even tighter grip. Her body quivered in excitement and relief.

"There you go, missy! And relax, it's non-alcoholic!" she said, shoving a cider into my hand, "Ah! I missed you!"

"Thanks. But you didn't have to!", I said as I took a sip. I have to admit! I almost forgot how cider tasted. But, what captivated me even more, was the beguiling smile of Rina. She was probably the only one in the entire room genuinely happy about my return.

"Are you kidding me? What better way to say that Kiara Sen is back in town and back to business?!", she enthusiastically said while signaling everyone to raise their glasses in excitement.

The crowd roared in agreement. Back in the day, I would have loved the very sight of such excitement under one roof. I would have lit the cigarette and enjoyed countless martinis in the company of men and women whose names I would forget by the break of dawn. But things were different now.

After the usual warm-up-chit-chat over the cider, I slowly proceeded to convey my plans to Rina.

"Rina ...there is something I have to tell you," I whispered into her ear. "It's about my book!"

"Oh! Yes! Speaking about your next book, I have a surprise for you. Be right back!" she whispered back before disappearing into the crowd.

Surprise? What can be more surprising than a surprise party?

Soon I was surrounded by a group of people interested in small talk and smiles. Have I mentioned I was claustrophobic?

Before the questions poured in, I excused myself, rushed to the bedroom, and closed the door behind me in angsty. I am what you call - A woman of few words. Ironic! I know. A bestselling author who prefers not to use her words and rather hide away from the mere possibility of having to use them. My bedroom seemed like the best place to hide till the party fizzled out. But little did I know I was not the only one in there.

"Umm ...you must be Kiara!"

I heard a voice behind me say. I turned around to follow the voice as my eyes met the most alluring pair of hazel eyes I had ever seen. It belonged to a tall, caramel-skinned man who seemed to walk straight out a fashion catalog. His raspy voice matched his rugged build adorning a denim jean and a loose white shirt. His soft black curls complimented his look, and a slight smirk on his lips made him all the more appealing. He was beyond charming, and for a second, all I heard was radio silence. So much so I could feel my heartbeat thumping hard in my body. I looked at him with utmost bafflement as the noise drew closer and closer from a distance.

"Hi! My name is Raul. Uh, sorry! I let myself in. I am not huge on parties, and this seemed to be the only lonely and safe corner in the house."

So he was a loner like me. But why was I even thinking that?

"Yeah …it's not a problem ...Hi! I am Kiara! I am sorry but, I don't think I know you," I said, trying to put the sentences together. I am usually good with faces, but for the love of God, I could not remember his. A man of his stature and look would have been an easy one to recall.

"Yeah, it's because I am your new ghostwriter!"

CHAPTER 3

"Excuse me?" I said, astounded by the revelation, "My ghostwriter? I ...what? I do not need a ghostwriter. I wrote my books!"

"Exactly, wrote! Now I am going to write for you," he replied in a condescending tone. A tone that did not sit well with me. Moreover, the audacity.

I could feel the air around me turn cold with every word we exchanged. First impressions aren't shit, and this was a perfect example.

"Oh! You found my surprise!" said Rina entering the room, "Kiara! Meet Raul! He is your …"

"Ghostwriter!" I said, cutting the introduction short, "Can I have a word with you?"

I pulled her out of the room and stared at her in utter disappointment. Resentment, anger, agitation….call it whatever you want, but I was feeling it all at that very moment.

"What were you thinking, Rina?" I said, letting go of the grip I had on her, "Where is Sana? You can't blame her for what happened, you know! I want to talk with her. It's what I was trying to tell you earlier. I can fix this! The publication will understand. Get her on the phone."

"Kiara! She quit!" she yelled back at me. "She quit! And you want to know why? Because of you! Your epic meltdown on national television was more than what she could handle. I am sorry, Kiara, but a lot has changed since you left. There is no one else to clean up your mess now but for me!"

Rina sighed in frustration and stormed away. I watched her get engulfed by the sea of happy drunk people.

I used to be happy like those people. Happy from intoxication with a carefree heart. But that was in the past. Rina was right! She was all that I've got. Sana quitting did not catch me by surprise as I had expected it. She always knew how to walk away from a mess, and in this case, I was the mess. It wouldn't have made sense for her to get dragged along my downfall.

I walked back into the room only to find Raul going through my books on the shelves.

"I ...uh …Rina and I," I stammered as I tried to collect my emotions together. Raul quickly turned and shot a comforting smile while holding the first edition of my second bestseller - *She Crawled Back Into The Woods*

"You don't have to explain. I am here to help you with your book and nothing else," Raul said, returning his gaze to the book and skimming through the pages. "Your personal life has nothing to do with me, and I don't want to make this any harder than it already is."

I smiled in relief as I moved closer to take my book from him. To my surprise, he turned to face me, and I tripped by mistake. I grabbed a part of the shelf for balance, forcing him to lean back against it. My eyes moved down from my hands on the shelf to his eyes and slowly his lips …his mellow looking lips. I was inches away from them, and I couldn't help but notice that the air around me had started to smell of strong musk. One whiff and I could feel my blood traveling through my veins. As much as I wanted, I couldn't move a muscle. I just stood there balancing on the shelf as his warm breath touched my cold body.

A roar from the party broke the sire, and I was quick to move away.

"Sorry! I lost balance, and I …"

"I know. It's alright! I am just not used to a woman falling for me like that," he chuckled as he gave the book in my hand and headed straight for the door. Before he exited, he turned to look at me one last time and said,

"It was nice meeting you, Kiara! Perhaps you will consider Rina's proposition, and we can discuss it better once you have made up your mind. I am probably what you never knew you wanted."

He winked with a playful smile and headed in the direction of the party. As he walked away, I couldn't help but notice this unfamiliar feeling building inside me.

Wait! What just happened?

CHAPTER 4

I woke up to the sound of a heavy downpour of rain. The windows let in a gleam of grey light that managed to cover part of my bedroom floor. I stared at the window sill where droplets were making their way through the tiny cracked hole into the bedroom wall. A heavy sigh gave away as I reached out to my phone and reluctantly stared at the bright screen.

5:30 am!

Last year's version of me would have jumped at the chance of opening up a beer saying it's 5:30 p.m. somewhere and guzzled down the entire case without a second thought. I would have then proceeded to write some gibberish and try to sell it off as a book.

That version of me was fun! That version of me thought she had the whole world figured out! That version of me was broken!

My phone suddenly beeped, interrupting my train of thought.

REMINDER: Meeting with John at 8 am

I kept the phone down for recharging the battery and continued to stare at the droplets. I felt like a stranger in my own house, and for the very first time, I missed my room at the center. It was a congested one with just a single bed and a table, unlike the spacious bedroom with imported tiles I was in currently. It was pure luxury in comparison but also the loneliest. At least people were walking around the corridors all the time there. Sometimes it was nurses on night watch, at times patients suffering from insomnia, and most of the time, it was just the janitor. I didn't have friends there, but the mere thought of their existence beyond my room gave me a sort of relief.

Soon enough, it was 8 in the morning, and I was drinking hot chocolate at my favorite coffee shop called Puzzles in Hauz Khas village. The rain seemed to have taken a slower pace, but the streets were still damp and muddy. For a writer, this is a scene of utmost serenity; The clove-scented air, the glass wall clouded with water droplets, and the warmth of a hot cup of cocoa.

"Hey, Champ!"

I jumped at the sound of the familiar husky voice. There stood John right before me in his usual air jordans, plaid shirt, and his spiky hair now neatly combed to the side, revealing his handsome face and ever so shiny forehead. One look at him, and I knew it was all Rachel's doing.

"John! Oh My Gosh! I missed you so much!" I said, throwing my arms around him. It felt so good to see him after what felt like forever. He hadn't aged a day. The same dimpled cheeks, the sharp jawline, and a happy smile; A smile that radiated positivity like no other. John was my childhood friend too, and we grew close for having been in the same neighborhood near Dwaraka. He was what you would say - the boy next door and a keeper. That always raised eyebrows and speculation by people around us about our relationship. Fortunately for us, we never saw each other in that light and protected the bond that we had at all costs. Every girl deserves a platonic guy best friend, and he was mine. Moreover, this saint of a guy was lucky enough to be touched by the arrow of cupid long before I had even considered taking on a serious relationship. Rachel was the love of his life and now his amazing wife. They have been happily married for three years now. Was there a part of me that envied him? Yes! But a major chunk of my heart felt nothing but happiness for him.

"So, how is Rachel?" I said, signaling the waiter for the menu, "I haven't seen her since ...you know!"

"Go ahead! You can say it ...", said John playfully, "How long are you going to put off the word *wedding* from your vocabulary?"

Suddenly I felt a strong pull in the pit of my stomach. My excitement hit the curb, and I could feel my body turning cold one long breath at a time. I pulled down the sleeves of my sweater to cover my trembling hands. It was late January in Delhi, and I wanted to blame the un-reliable weather for what I was feeling. But like John said, How long was I going to evade what happened?

John noticed my uneasiness and quickly shifted the topic,

"Rachel is doing great. She started a new job with the production house, and she is mostly tied up there. You know we both tried to contact you profusely. But..."

I involuntarily cut in,

"I didn't want to face anyone. I had dragged the situation to hell, and you guys along with it. The least I could do was save you both from any more unwanted media attention." I said, avoiding his eye contact and slowly gathering my emotions to ask what I was dreading the whole time,

"How is Jake?"

"Way better than how he was when you left him at the altar!"

CHAPTER 5

The rain had finally come to a halt and the skies were getting clearer at every turn of the lane. As I studded down the muddy pavement, my mind seemed to be the one getting clouded this time but with all the memories.

"I haven't been in touch with him that much as I used to. It just felt like I was picking sides, and it wasn't fair for him or you. Last I heard, he was planning on being a celebrity guest for some show they are shooting in Paris." John mentioned before he hurriedly left the cafe for a board meeting regarding the IT company he headed.

He was right! It just wasn't fair for him or me. But the guilt never left me. Memories of Rachel, John, Rina, Sana, and myself sitting at the Puzzles and fighting over samosas and hot chai during October rainy days now seemed like a distant one or something born out of a visual hallucination while writing a book. I was just 18 at the time and freshmen at that. None of us knew what was in store for us or how grey everything would be in a couple of years.

Before I knew it, I was already at Rina's lane, and I could smell her signature meatloaf to the end of the street. Her time abroad at all the culinary schools did serve her well. She co-owned a French restaurant in Delhi and an Indian one with her cousin in Paris. Now isn't that the best excuse to keep traveling between the two fabulous cities? I was nothing but always proud of her endless achievements. As I approached the front gate, I couldn't help but stare at the huge house that once used to shelter me from all the media attention. Rina would step out and give everyone an earful if they dared enter her property. Once, she went as far as hitting a photographer with a frying pan who had crossed her fence.

"Have you brought your white flag? Or should I come out with a frying pan?" a voice came out from the doorway. Rina was standing at the front steps with her arms crossed and a disappointing expression on her face.

I smirked as I climbed the stairs leading to her and said, "The only thing I have that's white on me is my bra. Are you sure you want me to take it off?"

She burst into laughter, threw her arms around me, and headed me in the direction of her kitchen to attack and devour her delicious meatloaf.

"So, what do you think of Raul?" Rina asked while cleaning the heap of dishes in the sink. "He is not like the other writers, you know? He helps and works closely with his clients from start to finish. All his previous clients managed to become bestsellers despite the long hiatus. I hope it works for you too."

"Rina! I don't need a ghostwriter! Moreover, I don't know where I stand when it comes to writing another book. I …"

I spoke in between my meatloaf bites.

"Stop It! Stop with the brooding. Hollans Publications gave you a book deal for three books, and this is your last one. If you're not handing over the manuscript in six months, they are certainly suing you." said Rina scornfully, "Raul is all you got now! And besides, Shreya approves of him. So pucker up and get on with it." said Rina putting the last piece of the washed dish back to its place in her vintage cupboard.

The woman had a point. They may not sue me, but I would have to let go of all royalties and payback even more for terminating the contract. Shreya was my editor. She was a kind woman, but never when it came to deadlines and finance. Getting on her wrong side was as good as hell. I would be broke with nothing in hand. The hard work of all these years would go down the drain, and not to mention the bad reputation that came along with it. The industry was ready to chew and spit me out as a 'has been', for a long time now, and here I was even considering giving them that opportunity on a golden platter.

If I screwed this up, I would be doomed. I signed up with Hollans four years back, and it was time to hand over the last book. My hiatus caused them a lot of money, and this was the only form of revival.

"Give Raul my number and ask him to call me tomorrow," I said, heading towards her fridge and searching for soda. A year and a half since I visited this house and, everything is still the same, even her selection of soft drinks in the refrigerator.

"Oh! I already did. He is meeting you at the Evergreen ranches at 10 in the morning." she winked as she breathed a sigh of relief on seeing her clean kitchen. Her sense of accomplishment was oozing out from her smile.

"That's an odd place to meet, and that's practically on the outskirts of Delhi," I said, opening a can of coke when my eyes suddenly fell on an off-white envelope on the kitchen counter with a familiar emblem, "Rina! What is that?"

Rina looked flustered at the mention of my newfound discovery. She was quick to pick it up and throw it in a pile of newspapers kept under the sink. I looked at her in astonishment.

"Rina! I am standing right here! I saw that!" I said, quite bewildered by her sudden behavior.

"Okay, fine! It's a job offer," she said, moving her chair closer towards me, "from Paris. There is a cooking show which I would be hosting with a celebrity. It's for a month, and I am supposed to leave in a week. I wanted to tell you once you were all settled in."

"Oh, My God! Rina! That's great. I am so happy for you!" I said, giving her a tight hug, "Your dreams are finally coming true! Remember how you kept mentioning hosting a cooking show one day back when we were in uni? Look at you now!"

But she did not seem to be as excited as I expected her to be. She looked down and reached for my hand. She held it tight and uttered in the most upsetting tone,

"The celebrity I am hosting the show with is ...Jake."

CHAPTER 6

I couldn't get myself to fall asleep. So I tried reading a book, but I couldn't focus. I tried watching videos on Youtube, but that didn't help either. I then tried counting sheep, but I just got the urge to google more about sheep instead. I finally gave up and headed to the kitchen to make myself a warm cup of tea. As I watched the water boil in the kettle, my mind began to wander, and before I knew it, I was thinking of Jake again. His stubble, his jet black eyes, and the way he called my name. He had a charm about him that made saying *no* a difficult task. So I definitely couldn't blame Rina for accepting his helping hand. He might not have been a good boyfriend, but he certainly was the best friend one could ask.

"I am sorry, Kiara. Jake was doing this show, and he knew how much I always wanted this opportunity as well. So he pulled some strings and put in a word with the casting directors. I only knew about it once I passed the audition. Please don't think I am a bad friend. You know I am always on your side."

Rina was genuinely upset with the whole ordeal. Honestly! It shouldn't be this hard for everyone. We were all close friends at one point in time.

"Just because it didn't work out between us...doesn't mean you have to pick sides or ice him out. I am glad he was thoughtful enough to help you out, and you were smart enough to seize the opportunity. I want nothing but the best for you Ri!" I said as I gave her the warmest of hugs, "You deserve the world!"

Rina seemed to have felt more at ease after the hug. She was glad I approved of it, but what she didn't realize is that my mind had started to slowly open the door I had forced shut all these months during therapy. It wasn't her, or for that matter, anyone else's fault. But the mind is a powerful thing, and no door is ever fully shut in the head.

I liked him. Perhaps, loved him too.

There was a gust of wind blowing through the windows, and I could see the highway like a bed of black velvet illuminated by the moonlight. The clock struck five and marked the arrival of dawn. I sipped clean the last few drops of the Moroccan tea and crawled back to bed. Giving up on any probability of sleep I

slowly unlocked the phone and opened Instagram to @jakematthew - a public verified actor profile with over 5 million followers.

A sense of relief and anxiety had filled my body. As I scrolled down the page, I noticed that he had taken off most of our pictures but forgotten this 3-year-old picture from the Evergreen Ranches. It was our fifth date, and he had surprised me with a white horse. His way of telling me that he was my prince on a white horse, like in the stories I believed. It was a perfect day. We rode the horse for hours. Did I mention I love horses? Beautiful creatures with the warmest souls. We watched the sunset later and had dinner at a private table in Le Broche. I always admired Jake's ability to switch up the atmosphere and keep anything interesting. An actor's charm, I believed. But that day, he was peculiarly excited. I had about two glasses of wine, and I was just about to order dessert when the waitress bought my favorite tiramisu with a bright sparkly thing on top.

It was a ring; A beautiful diamond ring.

The next thing I know, Jake was on his knees and professing how much he loved me.

"I knew you were the one the first time you walked through the doors in French class."

No, you didn't!

"My heart leaped out of my chest, and I knew it... She was the one."

But we barely knew each other.

"I love you so much, Kiara!"

But Sana loves you more.

"Make me the happiest man on earth by being my wife!"

He said, fastening the ring on my finger. *I don't remember saying yes!* I don't reckon he even asked the question. Everything happened in a matter of seconds.

He planted a kiss on my lips as the restaurant guest and staff cheered and roared in excitement. He resumed his seat opposite me with a sparkle in his eyes and the biggest smile I had ever seen on him.

He was happy!

I was confused!

But his happiness almost made me believe that this could work. There was no going back from this. *Or was there?*

I ordered my third glass of wine for the first time that day, and the alcohol intake never stopped.

"Quick! Let's commemorate this moment with a picture," said Jake handing over his phone to the waiter. He hugged me tightly from behind and directed my hand with the diamond ring towards the camera.

"Smile, baby! It is the best day of our lives!"

Perhaps it was the excessive alcohol or the joy of seeing an excited Jake. I wore the brightest of smiles on my face on his nudging.

The picture now smiled back at me, judging my soul and my motives in life.

587,902 likes

23,880 comments

There were a lot of comments under it. Some old but mostly new ones, horrible ones, pinpointing my mistakes and how better off he is without me.

For once, I agreed with the trolls too.

My fingers didn't stop scrolling through the sea of hate comments until the phone let out a notification ring.

It was a message from Raul.

"You up? It says last seen 5 mins ago."

"Yes, I am. What do you want?"

"I can feel the cold through the phone, ice princess! Trust me! I don't bite! Haha!

I couldn't sleep either. So I thought it would be a good idea to meet early. Up for it?"

"Sure! Meet you at Puzzles in 30 minutes."

"Great! By the way, do you like horse riding?"

CHAPTER 7

The sky looked like candy floss. The sun was about to rise, and the air was fresher than ever. The rain seemed to have finally stopped, and the road glistened at the aftermath. It was a good thing I layered up with a pink hoodie, blue jeans, and white converse. My look was casual, but it kept me warm from the ever-changing Delhi climate. And it was getting colder by the minute that morning. As I walked into the cafe, the familiar whiff of caffeine invited me with open arms. Joseph was working on some new specialty coffee beans for the new menu. I have known him and his wife right from my college days. Back in freshman year, we always huddled here in the corner booth during winters and worked on our term projects. He would give us refills for free, saying,

"Promise me you will come back when all of you become famous hotshots of the city. Okay?"

We used to nod back in approval. Years later, some of us managed to keep our promise. Joseph usually ran the early morning shifts at Puzzles, and it was always a delight to chat with him.

"Hello, Ms. Sen! I feel like I haven't seen you in ages. What brings you this early to Puzzles?"

“Oh, please! Joseph bhayya! Please call me Kiara like you usually do.”

“Okay, okay, beti. Just as you say. Shall I get you the usual, or would you like to try this new specialty coffee that I have been experimenting with?”

“Sure! I haven't had much sleep. So I could use some.”

Joseph smiled and proceeded to make some strong Chemex.

“I am supposed to meet Raul here. Do you know him? tall, dark, and know it all?”

Joseph giggled at my description.

“Yes! He is a regular here. Comes in every day and works in that corner booth right there,” he said, pointing to the cozy spot next to the window, “Yes! The spot that you and your friends used to encroach during winters, years ago. You can see him

typing his life away on that laptop of his. Nice kid. Very cheery and always with a smile. I knew his mother too.”

“Oh! I didn’t know you guys were that close,” I said, sipping the hot Chemex coffee Joseph placed on the table. “I thought he was new in town.”

“No, kiddo. Raul’s parents separated many years ago. His dad owned a part of the ranches a while back. But after his father’s death, his mother moved back last year to take care of the land with him. Heard they were in Banglore before this," said Joseph cleaning the coffee machine, "give him a chance, kiddo. He is a nice guy."

"Anything for you, Joseph bhayya." I smiled slyly.

I soon heard the cafe door ring open, and the sound of footsteps grew nearer. I turned around to find a very familiar face looking even more charming that gloomy morning. A white tee with a FILA jacket, black jeans, and red FILA shoes added to his charm. The man was handsome and knew how to work it in his favor. But it was his cheeky smile and hazel eyes that always caught my attention.

"Ready?"

"Are we going to ride horses?"

"Nope ...we are going to write your love story!"

CHAPTER 8

I sat beside Raul in the car as he drove up the hill towards Evergreen Ranch. The air was cold, but the view kept me warm. I looked up at him as he drove cautiously with strong attention on the road. This was honestly nice.

My eyes ran again from his hands on the steering wheel to his chiseled jaw and lips. He was very handsome for words.

His eyes suddenly met mine, and I was quick to look away. I could feel him acknowledging my awkward moment with a smile.

"Do you like me, Kiara?"

What?! Why is he asking that? Did he pick up on something? Was I staring that hard? My mind ran in all corners as I picked up words to reply.

"I mean, are you agitated by the fact that I am ghostwriting for you. Most of my clients instantly connect with me and talk about their ideas, but you have been giving me the cold shoulder from the start."

Phew! I sighed in relief and answered with a smile.

"Well, I don't hate you, If that is what you meant. I am just used to writing on my own. But, Rina is right. I do need your help. I didn't mean to give you the cold shoulder. I just had too much going on in my head."

"Well, that's why I am here." He looked at me for a second and gave out a smile. A smile so bright, it warmed up my soul. "What do you want to write? Do you have anything in mind? Fiction? Non - fiction?"

"Fiction!" I was quick to confirm. "A fictional love story, of course. Love stories sell best."

"Wow! Love stories sell," he repeated my line and laughed wildly. "Is that the reason you write about love? Don't you believe in love?"

"Nope."

Raul halted the car and looked towards me in surprise. "Kiara! Are you telling me that you have been writing this long without the slightest belief in love?"

"No need to be dramatic about it. Love is subjective. And love can be of many forms. But do I believe in true love between partners? No."

Raul shook his head in disbelief as he restarted the car and drove it to the parking point of evergreen ranches.

He remained silent for the next 10 minutes as we walked to the horse ranch. Did I piss him off? But having come from a family that dealt with separation, shouldn't he be as skeptical as I was? Or maybe I am too cynical for my good!

We were soon at the stables. The watchman helped us with the horses, and soon enough, we were both mounted on two of the gorgeous horses on the ranch.

I looked at the sky in happiness and down at my beautiful horse. I missed this. Suddenly a voice broke out from behind me.

"I have to ask. Is it because of Jake?"

Great! He didn't sound pissed at all. I turned towards him and shook my head in disapproval. I didn't want to continue this conversation, and I hoped he understood that. To my relief, he did. He just smiled and looked away.

He knew I was lying. The unspoken words seemed to have filled the air along with the sound of the horse-hoofs gracing through the grass.

In an attempt to pierce the crisp air with his heavy voice, Raul screamed in my direction,

"I am going to write your love story!"

CHAPTER 9

"Raul! Stop it!" I tried kicking his feet under the table but hit my foot on the table leg instead.

"Argh!" I shrieked at the sudden shock of nerves and attempted to pull my leg closer to my chair, but someone grabbed it to his side instead.

"Be still! Let me check. You bumped it too hard," said Raul, closely examining my leg while placing it on his sturdy thighs.

My face began to fluster by the way he held my foot and clasped it between his hands.

"Okay! You seem fine," he said, placing my leg back down, "Now! Where were we?"

It's been two weeks of endless brainstorming sessions at Puzzles over hot coffee and croissants. I ain't complaining, especially when Raul walks in through the cafe door every day looking breathtaking.

All the wandering eyes in the cafe halted collectively at his face adorned with soft curls. It was the same scene every day! More like a routine!

He would enter the door. Search around the cafe for me with doe hazel eyes and exclaim in a peculiar tone of excitement, "Kiara!" as he proceeded towards me.

I would welcome him with a beaming smile, small talk about the weather on how cold it's been getting, and slowly start plotting possible scenarios for the book.

I loved these sessions. It was a sight for sore eyes to see Raul work out the details in his pretty little head and stare back at me for approval. So much that I had become cautious the way I sat around him, talked to him, smiled at him. He was getting to me. Did he know that?

"Alright …alright. I am not bothering you anymore. Back to the story, the idea is good - Girl falls in love with a celebrity, he betrays her, and she gives up on love until she finds her Prince Charming." said Raul, as he scribbled the notes down on his book. The first half of the plotline had a familiar ring to it. But I was more surprised by how he didn't bother to question the authenticity of it all.

Come to think of it! He hasn't questioned anything since that day at the ranches.

"You make it sound …cliche! I need a twist." I proclaimed with an attempt to put his doubts, to rest if any.

"A twist?" he stared back inquisitively. His expression seemed to study mine.

"Yes. Something to get the readers intrigued." I said, cutting the tension and bringing my eyes back on the irregular writing on the pad, "A death or an open ending...something of that sort, you know?"

Raul looked back indecisively. I could tell he wasn't happy with my take on the twist. Probably judging my dark alter ego. I mean, the mention of 'death' did put a weird expression on his face. I should have probably been more sensitive after the talk I had about him with Joseph. Maybe he is thinking about his dad.

I slowly prepared myself for a wild response, but a smile burst on his lips and took me by surprise instead.

"Sure, as you say. Thanks for the notes. I will work on these and get back to you in a week. Would that be fine?"

I nodded back in approval. I think it was the fresh air or the adrenaline rush of starting a new book, but for the first time in a long time, I felt a bit at ease.

For the first time, I was excited to do something, and his smile was reassuring.

Raul's phone that was lying on the table beside me lit up all of a sudden with a text from a girl;

Rose

Hey, babe! Morning!

Last night was amazing. Let's do it again tonight.

CHAPTER 10

"Rina! Are you sure you need these many frying pans? You know you get them in Paris, right? And I am not sure they will allow you to use a worn-out one on the show." I said as I shuffled over the stack of utensils lying in her kitchen.

"That's the beauty of it! The production team and I will travel across Paris, learn every dish, and I will try to remake them by myself. So I do need those to depict that I try out recipes every day. Interesting, right?" she yelled back to me from the bedroom.

Rina's whole house was a mess at this point. Winter wear scattered all over the drawing-room floor, stacks of designer bags piled up on the sofa, cluttered jewelry on the dining table, and another stack of shoeboxes beside the recliner.

Muffy, Rina's two-year-old Chow Chow, kept running around the living room in despair.

"Muffy! Are you hungry? Kiara will feed you. Why don't you go to her?" Rina signaled to him while carrying a suitcase to the kitchen. Muffy bolted and was near her food bowl in seconds. He kept watching my every move as I slowly proceeded to remove a box of his favorite snacks from the top shelf and dump a quarter of it in his bowl.

Ten minutes later, the bowl was squeaky clean again.

"Are you sure you can babysit him thrice a week?" Rina questioned while trying to fit her new pair of shoes in her overstuffed luggage, "he can be a handful. My brother would have looked after him entirely if not for his interstate work trips every other day. Besides, I trust you with him more. I am sorry to have sprung this on to you last minute."

"You are doing me a favor." I gave small belly rubs to Muffy, who was lying half-dead on the floor, looking like he was intensely intoxicated, by the food he just devoured. His tongue flapped away from his mouth, and he growled in happiness from my touch. He was a cute one, and I adored him.

"The apartment was starting to feel lonely, and he is going to be a good source of entertainment. I can't be just working on the book all the time. So, how long is this show going to take?"

"Six months! Don't worry, Kiara! I will be back before you know it." she replied with an assuring smile. She managed to pack two ginormous suitcases and rolled them to the side of the sofa, "just a handbag is left!"

"So...what is Jake's role in all of this?"

There was a 2-minute pause, and I couldn't help but break the tension -

"Rina! I am not going to freak out. You can talk about him. You will be working with him after all, and we can't just dance around this topic. He is not Voldemort!"

I heard footsteps advancing towards the kitchen. Rina approached the kitchen table and slowly eased herself next to me. She pursed her lips and left out a slow sigh,

"I just... I don't want to make you feel uncomfortable in any way. If you have to know, Jake will be joining me at the end of every episode when I recreate the dish and will give his feedback, once he tastes it. He is just there to sell the show to the public. If things go well, we will get picked up for more seasons and will have a celebrity guest every season."

Honestly, I liked the concept of the show. I would have loved it more if Jake wasn't in it. But my personal opinions shouldn't matter here as it was Rina's show. Rina and Jake had always been good friends, and what Jake did for her by recommending her was admirable indeed. He did do a lot for the people he cared for.

For Rina's sake, I had to put on a happy front. After all that she had done for me, this was the least I could do. So I smiled back and exclaimed,

"Amazing, Rina! Can't wait to see it."

She smiled back in relief.

“Enough about me. Tell me about you! How is the book going? How is Raul? I see you’ve been spending quite a lot of time with him. Joseph gives me all the details every time I visit Puzzles. So, tell me! Tell me EVERYTHING!”

I chuckled at her excitement and her sly smirk but dismissed the cheerful mood quickly,

“Everything seems to be going great ...except ...”

“Except?”

“Except ...I think he has a girlfriend.”

CHAPTER 11

Hey Sana!

How are you?

Hope you are doing fine. I was hoping we could meet up for coffee. I got discharged from the rehabilitation center a few weeks back. I know it's been a

while, and there is so much to say. I know you might not want to see me after how we ended things last time. But I hope you still want to meet and talk things through. Because I do. I want to see you. I will wait for your response.

- Kiara

I stared at the mobile screen. My thumbs twitched between wanting to press *Send* and *Delete*.

I closed the app and proceeded to check her Instagram. @sanaty is now a private account with a small profile picture from the last trip we had taken to New York.

Twenty months without a call, message, nothing! After what I pulled that day, I wouldn't want to be my friend either. Crazy to reminisce there were days when we couldn't go without talking to each other for more than 48 hours. There would always be a "Hey, Bitch! Wassup" from either one of us to check on the living status of each other. But now, here I was contemplating on even sending a text.

Who would've thought life would turn upside down in a matter of a year and a half.

Sana used to be my publicist. But before all that, she was my best friend. I say "was" because that does seem like an eternity ago. Like a forlorn memory, I managed to hide perfectly in the folds of my memory book.

Sana and I had known each other since we were 8 when I had moved to Gurgaon from Central Delhi. I reckon running into the street to pick up a ball that rolled away from the house and lo behold! There stood a girl of my age in ponytails and skin as pale as the white dress she was wearing that day. She was my neighbor.

My parents were always away in their pursuit to close business deals while I spent my time at Sana's place, where her parents babysat me all year round. We went to the same school, same tutoring centers, and the same university with different majors. Miss Fernandez, Sana's mom, was more of a mother to me than my mother ever was.

While I pursued my interest in writing, Sana pursued her interest in public relations. It was like a match made in career heaven. She was my confidant for everything, from books to boys. And I was the same for her. So we thought!

I met Jake for the first time at Sana's house. I was helping her organize things for her first university field trip scheduled within the first week of classes when we heard a knock on the bedroom door. I turned to find this handsome man with sleek brown hair and a dimpled smile. I wasn't surprised when I later found out he was trying his hand at modeling and acting.

"Hey, Sana! I came to borrow the notes you had promised me. Your mom let me in!" he said, in a low voice while his gaze kept shifting between the two of us, "I am sorry if I interrupted something. I took permission from the hostel just for this."

"No worries, Jake! I was expecting you. Oh, by the way, that's my friend Kiara. She goes to our uni too. Majoring in literature."

Jake and I exchanged smiles and nodded in acknowledgment. He was too handsome for words because I remember not being able to take my eyes off him even for a second. Sana quickly gave him a notebook and sent him on his way.

"Who was that?" I remembered asking Sana excitedly, "He is so cute!"

"My classmate and my potential boyfriend.", Nina chuckled as she put her hand around me and directed me to the living room.

"Point taken!" I responded in support.

"So! Did you finish the book? Is the manuscript ready? I have pulled some strings in Holland Publications. I can't wait for them to read it.", she said, handing me a cup of coffee.

I gazed at her in gratitude. I have never felt more hopeful than that very moment.

"You don't know how much it means to me, Sana! I am excited and nervous. I came to give you the finished manuscript."

I handed a thick folder over to her,

"Do you think they will like it?"

"Of course, they will. Can you believe you are my first client!?" It will only go up from here. For both of us! You just wait and watch!

Kiara, the famous writer, and her publicist Sana. It's us against the world now."

She exclaimed as she went through the pages. She was right! It only went up from there until everything broke down.

SEND

Or

DELETE

The mobile screen kept blinking back at me. I took a deep breath and pressed SEND. I fell back to the bed with a swarm of lost thoughts when I was suddenly interrupted by a notification.

“Can we meet? I want to talk.”

It was a text from Jake.

CHAPTER 12

The steam from my fresh cup of coffee lingered around me as I stared blankly at the open text in front of me.

"Can we meet? I want to talk."

The last time Jake said, "I want to talk", we never ended up "talking". A month after our supposed wedding that never happened, I had received the same text at 12:30 am, and I was quick to respond out of guilt.

"Yes, do you want me to call?"

"No, I said I want to meet you. I am outside. Come out, Ki! I wanna see you."

Ki! He called me Ki only when he was drunk out of his mind. This man was at my doorstep, drunk at midnight. The very thought scared me, not because I feared him for who he was but for what I had done that had led to all this.

"Please, baby! I want to see you one last time."

I ran to the door and unlocked it in a hurry, only to find an intoxicated Jake standing in the hallway dressed in his casual black hoodie, black jeans, and sneakers. He could barely stand and kept leaning on the door frame.

“Ki! Baby! I missed you,”

He exclaimed while throwing his hands around my body and putting half his body weight on me in the process. He smelt of rum and cedarwood cologne. I had to admit I sure did miss the scent and his warm touch. But I was in no position to admit it, and he was in no state to ‘talk’ like he had claimed 5 minutes back on the text.

I slowly brought him to the couch, removed his socks, and handed over a glass of warm water to sober him up.

“Do you want me to make you some coffee?”

“No!”

“Jake! It will help you sober up!”

“No!”

“Jake! Please, you need to …”

I couldn’t finish what I intended to say as Jake had quickly shut me up by planting his lips on mine. The same warm feeling!

I slowly opened my mouth to let him in. I knew I would regret this, but I couldn’t stop. I craved for his touch as much as he needed mine.

He slowly removed my tee, removed his, kissed my neck, and held me in his arms to feel closer to my skin. It was his habitual way of initiating his love. One wouldn't believe he was drunk, but then again, the strength one gets when drunk is always something else.

"I missed you. I had to see you. Touch you. Feel you. I just had to Ki!"

He said, stopping his kisses midway, looking straight into my eyes, and cupping my face in his hands. His eyes glowed with passion in my dim apartment nightlights.

"I missed you too."

My response was so quick and involuntary that I didn't realize what was happening. But it seemed to have produced shockwaves on Jake's body, for he was quick to lift me, head to the bedroom, place me gently on the sheets, and hover over me while showering me with kisses. I did miss him. But not in the way he did.

As I tugged my hands on his hair while he felt my insides, I knew I had let lust win that night. It wasn't love! Just pure lust and the feeling of familiarity.

I woke up the next day to an empty bed and a note on the side -

Last night was a mistake.

I will never see you again.

- Jake

It's been a year and a half since that night. But why does it still feel like it happened just a few weeks ago? The text had started to evoke some unresolved emotions.

The rain is usually in a full storm during this time of the month, and today was no less. I had grabbed a cozy corner in Puzzles to work on some ideas and mostly to ponder over the biggest question of all - What do I text back to Jake?

"More coffee, Miss Sen?"

Joseph had just brewed a fresh jug of coffee. The aroma filled the air like a string of instant nostalgia. Years later, the cafe remained intact - the same pretty portraits on the wall, the same aromatic freshly brewed coffee, and the same warm smile from Joseph. At least something in this town remains the same.

"No, thanks! I am yet to finish the last cup."

Joseph smiled and proceeded to pour coffee to someone sitting in the other corner of the room, and I went back to staring at the text again. Just when I was about to give up and head home, a voice broke out from behind me -

"You are in my seat!"

I turned around to see a familiar smile and caramel-skinned handsome man with his bundled notes and a laptop. Raul was always a treat for sore eyes though he seemed tired himself. But his smile never failed to make me giddy and forget everything that I was thinking a second back. He had grown on me. His intense stare. His curls. His skin. His eyes. His lips. His kissable lips!

What?! Stop!

I forced myself to snap out of my thoughts and realized I was staring at him for too long. He reciprocated with a smile. Like he knew I was thinking.

"Hey! How is the writing coming along? I didn't get to proof-read chapter 7." I said, smiling while slowly running my hands along his arm, resting on the chair rim. Wait! Why was I touching him? I immediately withdrew my hands and signaled him to occupy the chair before me.

Damn. I should stop thinking about this man this much.

Or men, in general, maybe. It's been a while, and it's starting to show. I shrugged at my stupidity.

He gave a crooked smile at my weird expressions and threw himself on the other side. Phew! I guess he decided to look past that awkward moment.

"Well ...it's good I ran into you here. I did have some questions regarding the plotline."

"Like?"

"Like ...Why did Helen leave Liam at the altar? Why didn't she catch up on the red flags sooner? Was it her fault? Or did she do everything in the name of love or ..."

"From the fear of being alone."

CHAPTER 13

"You need to let loose a little Kiara!"

Raul had screeched this at the top of his lungs while working on a few plot line pieces at her apartment, "This sounds a bit boring!"

"How is this boring?"

"You are telling me that Helen forced Liam into this. That she spent literally hours together every day, created the greatest possible chemistry in textbook romance, made sweet love every other page, and Helen never felt a thing? Even for a second?"

"No."

"How?"

"It's just the way it is."

"I don't buy it. And if I don't buy it, your audience wouldn't buy it either. There must be a solid reason. Otherwise, please make Helen fall in love with him eventually."

"No! Not everything that looks like textbook romance eventually turns out to be the greatest chemistry in literature. Take Gatsby, for instance."

"That's just insane, Kiara. Gatsby died! Poof! Shot! Is that what you plan to do here? It needs to pan out well. It's a romance novel. Not a tragedy!"

"What's so tragic in learning to be alone? It's a good ending."

"No! It's boring! Change it up."

Raul was in no mood to budge, and nor was I. The apartment filled up with cold air. Maybe, from the tension between us, or it was the unpredictable weather. But amid all this, I still couldn't stop noticing how insanely attractive and wholesome the man that stood before me was, with his strong sense of judgment and strong chiseled jawline to match.

"Aren't you the one trying to sell love now?"

"No! With the way the story is going, I know the characters deserve a happy ending. I don't think you get my point!"

"Oh, is that so? Have it your way, then. Finish the damn book yourself. I never wanted to write it anyway!"

I glared back at Raul before hurriedly moving towards the door and slamming it shut behind.

Oh, how I could use a drink right now!

Delhi rains had gotten worse by the day, and the streets were slippery than ever. I paced myself gently to avoid a distorted fall in the muddied pavement.

What was Raul thinking?

Why get so mushy about this?

It's my book at the end of the day. If Helen wants to end up alone, she will end up alone. Who was Raul to make any assumptions about my characters?

It's not like it's taken from my real life.

Well, not entirely.

My brain ached with all the voices circling in my head. The scene of Raul's sad eyes staring back at her as they argued flashed before me. It was the first time we had argued, or I had ever seen him that motivated yet disturbed.

As suspected, the clouds broke out to heavy thunder and rain again. I instantly regretted not having taken my umbrella from the apartment. But being the pluviophile that I was, a little rain did me good at this moment. My head seemed to come down from the anxious high. I closed my eyes, looked up, sniffed the moist air, and smiled at the cold droplets that fell on my face in slow movements. It felt good.

"Uhh …so …do you want the umbrella or not?"

I opened my eyes to the direction of the voice and found a sweaty Raul panting from having followed me out with the umbrella on the first sight of rain.

I couldn't help but feel a bit guilty for the way things transpired. So I ran towards him and took the remaining space under his umbrella for refuge.

"I am sorry for bursting out at you like that."

I said as I moved closer to him till his warm breath fell on my cold skin. He put my hands around me, pulled me closer in a warm embrace, and instantly changed the subject,

"This would have been a perfect scenario for two characters in love to kiss. Don't you think?"

"The cliche kiss in the rain," I chuckled while we slowly turned and proceeded towards my apartment, "except we aren't in love."

"Not yet," Raul whispered into my ear that sent a chill down my spine until my legs.

I turned to look him in the eye to question his sudden revelation but was met with his free hand behind my head as he pulled me closer and forced my lips to gently graze his. I jolted and moved back for a second, but he eagerly pulled me in for deep seconds. It wasn't a gentle graze anymore. I felt him as his hand slowly moved from my head to the waist while he still managed to hold the umbrella with the other. I pulled him closer and continued to convulse on his lips with passion. It took him a minute to break apart from me and utter,

"Not there yet!"

CHAPTER 14

"Kiara! What?! Omg! Tell me everything," an excited Rina squealed at the dessert aisle of the supermart, "I knew it! I knew you guys would hit it off! So glad I get to witness this just before I leave."

"Shhhh, Rina!" I signaled her to lower her voice. But she couldn't contain her excitement and kept adding desserts to her cart.

"For Celebrating this! A little sugar never hurt anyone," she winked as she added the third box of Betty Crocker Cookie Dough to the mix.

Rina was leaving Delhi tomorrow for good, and we decided to have a last-minute run to the mart to make sure she got everything.

"Muffy is going to miss you!" I sighed heavily, "And so will I!"

"Oh please!" remarked Rina with a hint of sarcasm, "You've got Raul now! Did you guys speak after that hot make-out session?"

Rina nudged me with her elbow to get more details out of me, "Tell me! Tell me! Tell me!" she continued to whine.

"Well, he got a call right after and said he would meet up with me later today. So there isn't much to say," I said, taking away the fourth box of dessert from the mix and returning it on the shelf. The woman was going overboard with sugar at this point.

"Okay! That's a turnoff," she exclaimed.

"Tell me about it. I think it's that girl who texted that day. Do you think I should ask him?"

I asked her inquisitively. The text Raul received that day had been at the back of my mind for a while, and now it seemed like it was clawing its way out for some answers. Part of my brain was still in a haze after the kiss, and part of it had gone back to my usual self-sabotage mode.

Why do I do this to myself?

"Kiara! I don't think he would have kissed if he wasn't single. I mean, he didn't seem like that kind of guy," Rina shot a smile back at me in reassurance.

"Let's see," I sighed harder this time and looked back at my neurotic friend, who was now busy tossing bundles of foil paper into the shopping cart.

I was going to miss confiding in this woman. Over the years, she had become my human version of a personal diary of sorts where I could dump all my feelings without being judged or reprimanded. In a way, my safe space.

I still remember the first time I met her at school when we were in grade 10. We were just 15! Little did I know she would be the one to stick in the long run - through the writer's block, the speed dating days, the messy breakups, the running away from the altar, the rehab, and figuring out my life. And now here she was all set to fly to Paris and chase her dreams. I was so proud of her, but I couldn't help but feel a little pang in my gut at the same time. It must be because of her departure or the fact that she would be spending the next six months talking to Jake with my topic seldom coming up. Or maybe it's the fact that she has got her life under control, unlike me. Numerous factors, but I seem to remain the root cause of my problems.

Rina was checking all the items out and began rambling,

"Come on! I will drop you home. Sleep in after meeting Raul. You have to meet me at the airport early in the morning. It's already 6 pm."

"I will be there, Rina. Don't worry!"

It was 7 pm, and I had already redone my apartment thrice, paced over seven times, and contemplated whether to light a scented candle over nine times. It wasn't Raul's first time at the apartment, but this time it seemed different. I rehearsed and re-rehearsed multiple scenarios but in vain. My anxiety was getting the best of me with sweaty palms and mad adrenaline.

I had made pasta for dinner and bought sparkling cider for a nightcap.

7:30 pm and still no sign of Raul. Did he regret the kiss? Is this too soon? Is he seeing that other girl?

To make matters worse my brain decided to remind me of the text from Jake, which was still left unanswered.

Just when my mind had begun to run wild, my phone began to ring, and to my relief, it was Raul.

"Hey! I was waiting for you…"

I tried my best to sound calm and composed.

"Kiara, I am sorry I wouldn't be able to make it. It's a family emergency," Jake spoke at the other end of the line with a tone of guilt and dismay.

"Oh, okay."

It was my turn to speak in the same tone.

"Raincheck?"

"Sure, Bye. Take care, Raul."

I hung up in angst. He was avoiding me, and I began to feel like a fool for having expected something more to happen.

There was no logical explanation for what I did next, but I felt a weird rush to do so.

"Jake! Meet me in an hour at our usual place."

CHAPTER 15

"Hello, mam! I just wanted to check if the location is correct," said my Uber driver while activating the ride on his mobile, "Connaught Place, right?"

I nodded in approval, and the Uber kick-started the long ride from my apartment to C.P.

50 minutes!

I sighed, looking at the watch, and looked out the car window. There was a charm to Delhi after 8 pm. The sea of people returning home after a long day at work, the foggy lamp posts leading them home, the hustle and bustle!

Sure was better than just staring at trees from the room at the rehabilitation center. That place might have helped me, but it was also the loneliest couple of months I had ever spent. Just the sight of a busy street was a bit more calming than the trees.

I couldn't help but start thinking of Raul, the desperation in the sound of his voice, and the way he was quick to hang up.

Was it an emergency?

Perhaps he was avoiding her?

He might have realized that it was a mistake, just like how Jake did that morning.

But wasn't he the one who initiated the kiss?!

I was slowly getting tired of men in my life initiating contact and regretting later.

I must be some sort of an omen.

Maybe that's why it never works out with anyone.

Sana's voice kept ringing in my ears.

"Why are you so scared of being alone?" she had once asked while rearranging the sheets of the contract in order, "Why do you think you need someone to pull you up ...let alone survive?"

That was about three to four years back when I had just launched my first novel, and it was doing pretty badly on the charts. Desperately pacing to and fro in Sana's office, I was trying to come up with possible solutions to catapult the sales. A PR stunt seemed to be a good idea at the time.

How selfish!

"Sana! I can't explain, okay! I just - I just feel that associating me with some celebrity will do the trick. I mean, Hollywood and Bollywood do it all the time. Take two individuals who have the potential to be huge if put together and work your PR stunt magic." I beamed at her anxiously. I thought my world was about to crash and burn at the time.

Sana looked back at me in disapproval. She didn't like where the conversation was going. She nudged her head to the side as if she gave it another thought and replied,

"Kiara! It sounds good on paper, but listen! It is your first book, and it's set to launch in bookstores all over India in a matter of a month. You worked hard on this. It took us a year to get to this point, and I know you are pretty tired with this whole process but do you want people to focus more on your personal life than your book?"

She was right. It was a long journey, and things had changed drastically over the months. Sana had established her own PR company and was already handling some of the best talents in the industry. She might be right about the long journey, but not about the reluctance to associate me with one of her talents to create a newsworthy buzz that would, in turn, guarantee high book sales. I couldn't help but wonder whether it was fair for her to turn the idea down when I had nothing but rooted for her all the way, even when things weren't so great at my end.

Sana seemed to have figured out what ran in my head. She slammed the papers on the desk, fell back on her chair, took a deep breath, and said,

"Fine! Tell me! Who do you want to get associated with? I will put in a word and see."

"Maybe if you could ask Jake? I promise it won't be awkward. There will not be any PDA ...just some baseless rumors. Only if you are comfortable with it."

Sana stared back at me as if she had just seen a ghost.

"Jake?! You mean, my boyfriend?!"

CHAPTER 16

"We are here, Ma'am!"

I was woken up from my train of thought with a sudden jolt of the car. I got out and started walking around the block leading to Cha Bar cafe that was in connection with the Oxford bookshop. I could feel my jeans and tee getting heavy with every step.

Maybe I should go back?

Maybe all this is a big mistake!

But I continued to climb the steps leading to the cafe. I guess a part of me really did want to resolve this once and for all.

Cha-Bar used to be my favorite joint. I would spend hours writing and editing my pieces and drowning my sorrows and worries in their coffee. The walls of this place had seen more tears than the people who were there in my life. Somehow this place always seemed to give me clarity when I needed it.

I was early. There was no sign of Jake. So I decided to explore the bookshelves as a way to distract my anxious mind. There laid in a section in bold letters,

Bestsellers By Kiara Sen

It's been four years of living this infamous author life, but it never truly felt like my own. The picture of Kiara Sen that looked back at me from the *About The Author* profile was talented, egotistical, eccentric, and did anything to get her way. Might I add, an alcoholic too!

But the Kiara Sen that looked back at me was a broken, lonely, and an overall self-sabotaging soul.

I felt like I was looking at my alter ego, to put it rightly!

"That's one of my favorite pictures!"

I heard the familiar voice after what seemed like ages. It felt like coming home yet a lonely one at that. I turned to find Jake standing before me in his usual jogging pants and hoodie. He still looked as handsome as the last time I saw him. But this time, he was in his right mind.

How do you address a former lover or fiancé? Would a hug be too personal or a handshake be too informal?

But a strong sense of emotion just took over me, and I couldn't help but hug him. He reciprocated with an even tighter one. He still smelled and felt the same.

I let go of my grip slowly and looked up to find his eyes still looking down on me with the same passion in his eyes, not a lustful one but an emphatical one.

"Jake, I am sorry," I said feebly, to which he immediately replied in the most melancholy voice I had heard,

"I know I am too."

Soon enough, we were at the corner booth looking down at our respective beverages with nothing but the tension between us. A tension so strong you could cut it with a machete. I observed the man sitting across me involuntarily.

The last two years were transformative for Jake. Prior to us getting together, he had only done a couple of side acting in commercials and some modeling gigs. But the news of our dramatic wedding that didn't happen kind of put him in the limelight. The media had taken kindly to the man's emotions after picturing me as the runaway bridezilla that broke his heart. Sponsors were quick to chime into his infamous position and soon, he was landing roles in series, shows, and even managed to do two blockbuster movies.

"Jake Matthew! The Boy Who Rose From The Ashes."

I once read his interview with this headline in a newspaper in the cafeteria at the rehabilitation center.

He spoke about his past projects and his upcoming ones, but never about his damaged love life. He would always politely respond, “I loved her, and I still do. Love is not a bad thing. Sometimes things work out, and sometimes they don't. It’s no one’s fault. She will always have a special place in my heart, and I am always grateful for everything!”

Jake was a humble one, and that’s one of the many qualities I liked about him. He deserved all the good that came his way.

“So, how is life after rehab?”

Jake decided to take the plunge.

“I thought about visiting you a couple of times. But I, you know, after the whole wedding day fiasco and that night too ... I...”

“No, I understand,” I interrupted “I am doing fine. I am working on the final book and keeping myself busy. How about you? I heard you are joining Rina and the production crew in Paris.”

“Yeah ...yeah! I have some film projects there too.”

“That’s amazing, Jake! You are doing so good for yourself.”

He laid back on the chair and began fidgeting the spoon. I could see he was uneasy with the entire ordeal, and he was refraining from saying something to me.

“What is it?” I questioned and reached out for his hand. He was quick to push it away and immediately blurted out,

“Why did you do it?”

“Do what?”

“Leave me on the wedding day like that? Why? Was it the religion issue? Was it me? What was the reason? Because you just left me standing there high and dry. Standing there all embarrassed! I want to know, Kiara! What did I do wrong for you to run away from me like that? I spent days and nights wondering where I went wrong. I have done nothing but be faithful to you. All you ever kept telling me was, “It’s not meant to be.” Such bullshit!”

At this point, Jake’s voice began to rise with each sentence. The barista peeped from the counter to see if everything was fine, and I immediately signaled him in a positive manner to avoid any suspicion. I looked back at a confused Jake and took a deep breath-

“What I did to you was unfair! I know that! I wasn’t ready, Jake! I never was. And it was wrong of me to take you away from Sana in the first place. Our relationship was built on a lie. It was never supposed to last. I made you break her heart. She was my best friend, and I ruined her."

"I chose you, Kiara!"

"And that was wrong, Jake. She loved you so much."

"Didn't you love me?"

"I don't know."

"What?"

I didn't know. That was the truth! I never knew how love felt. If I did love Jake, I would have been happily married by now and celebrating our second anniversary. But here we were, sitting across the table from each other like mundane strangers.

"Jake, listen ...I…"

Before I could say anything, he got up to leave. He clenched his fist in anger, and his voice wasn't melancholy anymore,

"I can't do this, Kiara! It took all the energy I had to do this, but clearly, I was wrong. Sana was right about one thing, though. You are just a lonely girl who loves breaking people to get what you want."

CHAPTER 17

Hey!

Sorry about last Wednesday.

Are you there?!

Call or text me as soon as you get this.

-Raul

I read the text in a flash and immediately closed the phone and kept it inside my handbag. It's been two days since that night, and everything has gone downhill since then.

"Are you ready, Kiara?"

Dr. Nancy, my therapist, asked in a calming voice, to which I nodded immediately in assurance,

"Yes! Yes! Sorry, it was an important message."

I placed the handbag on the side of the recliner and eased myself comfortably into the chair. I would be lying if I said I was completely prepared for this. I have been skipping therapy for the last six weeks. After all that went down last week, I needed to talk to someone about everything - Rina leaving for Paris, the euphoric moment with Raul, the ridiculous aftermath, the awkward conversation with Jake, everything!

"I am glad to finally meet you, Kiara! I heard a lot of good things about you from Miss Rose. I have read your books too. They are quite remarkable." said Dr. Nancy while handing over a cup of coffee to me. She was unlike Miss Rose. They were the same age, but the aura of the two were poles apart. Dr. Nancy looked like someone who had her priorities sorted out. Huge frames with her diplomas and achievements surrounded the cozy room. Random artifacts were lying all across the room, huge French windows to leave ample amounts of light in, a soft carpet on the floor, and a comfy sofa in one corner. Dr. Nancy sat across my recliner in a sturdy table with glasses on and a notepad to keep track of my behavior. Looking at how she was scribbling notes into it after every sentence I spoke, it felt like intense behavioral therapy.

"I am sorry I missed the past few sessions. I have been a bit caught up with everything." I replied, sipping the warm black coffee she had handed over to me earlier. "I needed this. Thank you for taking the time to see me."

"Most of the patients, from the rehabilitation center, take at least three months to come back to therapy. We usually recommend it immediately because you are still getting the hang of staying away from the addiction in the real world. Did you have alcohol in the last few weeks or an intent to have a little?"

"No! I haven't had any, but I did have the intent to have a sip last week. I...I have been having a hard week." I said, looking down at my fingers nervously. I had this habit of scratching my nails together when I am in confronting situations. This was no less.

"Kiara, take a deep breath."

Dr. Nancy could sense my uneasiness and reached out to my hand and patted it a little to comfort me.

"Now tell me, when was the last time you spoke to your mom and dad?"

"It's ...it's been over a year," I replied timorously.

"They never visited you in Rehab?"

"No, they never even tried."

I don't blame them either. Having an alcoholic daughter with dirty laundry aired in the public time and time again is not what any Indian parent wants. Growing up, my family was absent for most of my childhood because they were always busy traveling for business. I grew up in a household where I was closer to my nanny than my mom before she passed away several years ago. I hid behind my books and wrote my feelings. It was my only solace.

I never really wanted to be a writer. I wanted to be in production. But being a writer had more chances of getting that attention from my family, which I missed growing up. All I wanted for them was to be proud of their only daughter. Instead, they got a daughter who never kept up to their expectations and dragged their family name in the dirt.

As I sat there sharing all the intricate details about my relationship with my parents, Dr. Nancy pulled out a visitor sheet from my medical reports and looked back at me inquisitively.

"Didn't you say your parents never visited you in the rehab?"

"Yeah," I replied, addled.

"But, Kiara, your visitor sheet shows three visits from your mom."

CHAPTER 18

"Your mom! What?! Kiara …I had no idea. If I had known … Kiara, I never knew about her visits."

Rina stammered through the phone. The FaceTime might be pixelated, but her tone was crystal clear. I remember putting down just 3 names for the next-of-kin visitor permission slip - Rina, Mom, and Dad. I had put down my parents' names in case of an emergency and never in the hopes of seeing them. That was the last thing I wanted to push me to the edge of no return.

But did a part of me wonder if they ever thought of visiting their only mentally-unstable daughter in the vicinity of a rehabilitation center? Part of me did, but I killed those thoughts every time it popped to save myself from yet another disappointment.

"How do you feel about all this?"

"Don't ask! I feel like I am being dragged through hell. Everything seems to be going against me. I must be going through some karmic balance, I guess," I replied in a sarcastic tone though I firmly believed in every word I had just uttered.

"Listen to me! You are not a bad person. You just made some bad choices. That doesn't make you a bad person okay!" she said, trying to cheer me up, "Let's change the topic. What's up with Raul? You haven't talked or texted about him since the kiss. Did you guys talk?"

"I think that's going to be added to the list of bad choices. I don't think …"

My conversation was interrupted by the doorbell, followed by a few gentle knocks on the door.

"Oh! Someone is at the door! I think it's my Amazon order of all the funky stationery supplies I ordered."

Rina couldn't help but giggle at the happy shift in my tone.

"I haven't seen anyone get excited over a few pens and clips like you. Saved by the bell! Call you later then …bye!" she said and hung up.

Saved by the bell indeed!

Muffy was playing with his toys in the living room but got instantly triggered by the doorbell.

"Here, Muffy!" I directed him to the balcony and hurriedly unbolted the door with glee, only to find a dejected Raul standing in the hallway with a takeaway bag from Puzzles. White tee, blue jeans, white sneakers, and that gorgeous smile again. He shoved the bag into my face and tilted his head to one side to look at me like a wounded puppy. And to my dismay, it was working.

“Can I come in?” he asked while leaning forward and keeping one arm on the door sill, “Sorry I came unannounced. You weren’t texting me, and I felt really bad for blowing you off that day.”

“It's alright!” I said, letting him in, “Clearly, you had something better to do.”

The sarcasm didn’t sit well with Raul. He placed the takeaway bag on the coffee table and turned towards me. His eyes now beaming with regret but also exhausted from all the melancholic foreplay.

“I figured you’d be mad. If it’s any consolation, I wasn’t having a good time.”

He paused for a second and collapsed on the sofa with his head in his hands,

“I …I had to help my mom sell the farmhouse.”

“You are selling?” I asked, slowly nestling myself right next to him, “But why? I thought you loved that place!”

“I do! But my dad left us with a lot of debt when he passed away. And this was our only option. Ghostwriting is not a solid career, you know.”

His voice began to break, and his eyes welled up as he spoke every word out of his mouth. Like it pained him to pluck it and throw it out of his body.

"Sorry to hear that! But why didn't you ever start writing your own novels? I have seen your work. You are amazing! I mean …we wouldn't be working together otherwise." I said involuntarily, placing one hand on his thighs. It took me a second to realize it, but Raul didn't seem to notice.

"Because I never got a good story idea of my own. I was always good at spinning words for others, but not my own. So I began ghostwriting for authors, websites, screenplay writers, production houses, and so on. Maybe one day! For now, I am going to pay off all the debts and save the rest." he said, placing his hand over mine.

I guess he noticed after all. He clasped it and intertwined his fingers into mine slowly as I smiled back.

"Can I ask you something?" I said, positioning myself a bit more closer, "Are you seeing anyone? I mean …I know we kissed and I really enjoy your company. But are you?"

Raul smiled, leaned in, kissed my lips softly, and said,

"I wouldn't ever do what I just did if I was with someone else! Why do you ask?"

"I once saw a message pop up on your phone from some girl called Rose. I thought she was your girlfriend."

“She was. We dated for 2 years but broke up when I moved to Delhi. Things weren’t working between us anyways. I did meet her once, but it’s history. I have my heart set on this pretty caramel-skinned brunette now.” he said, winking at me and showing off his pearly whites again.

I could feel life pouring back into my veins. What a huge relief! This meant only one thing. Should I ask, or shouldn’t I? Will it be too high-school-ish if I did?

“What are you thinking?” he chuckled at my state of confusion, “Are you wondering if we are …”

“Yeah!” I blurted before he could finish the sentence.

Raul moved in closer. There it was again …the familiar musky scent and his hot breath. He slowly placed his lips on mine, and a second later, he went in deeper. His one hand ran across my hair, and the other held me by the waist tightly. With a swift pull, I was on his lap now, facing him and kissing him with passion, pushing my body closer to his and burning myself up...one push at a time. I faintly realized how his touch always managed to make me feel isolated from the rest of the world for a few minutes. Like, Magic. I said to myself.

He broke away from the kiss, placed his hands loosely around my waist, buried his head in the nape of my neck, and breathed heavily on my skin. He then looked up and slowly placed his eyes on mine. He replied in his sexy husky voice that fought to catch his breath,

"Yeah! We are!"

CHAPTER 19

"The story is coming out great! You will be so proud of me," he said, giving me a kiss and going back to staring at the screen of the laptop while casually sipping the hot cocoa I made for him. Muffy was lying by Raul's side, fully immersed in his periodic hair strokes at his back.

Maybe this is what "Easy Like Sunday Morning" by Lionel Richie actually means. My Sunday mornings never looked this great. Raul wrapped up in the corner of my bed, typing his heart away and discussing storylines with me. Semi-naked, might I add. I can get used to this!

"Alright! Let me make you some breakfast," he said, springing up from the bed and putting on his tee, "You must be hungry! You had very little to eat last night as well."

"Look at you! Rescuing me from hunger!" I said, giving him a warm kiss on the cheek before he proceeded to the kitchen, "Thanks, babe!"

Raul and I have been dating for the last 8 weeks, and everything has been going pretty well. Too well, actually. He spent most of his time at my place running storylines and working on the content. And I am not one to deny the fact that I loved spending all this time together. He was a marvelous cook, and he kept sweeping me off my feet with his improvised European dishes.

But we still haven't come close to discussing my past. Maybe Raul was being patient and giving me time, or perhaps he didn't want to open a can of worms that might send him running.

"A penny for your thoughts?" Raul said while making his signature French toast,

"you have been lost in thoughts the past few days."

"It's just ...I have been thinking about my parents a lot lately," I said, swirling my spoon in the cereal bowl, "I haven't spoken to them in over a year now."

"Hmm ...I think you should call them."

"You think so? I am confused."

"Yeah! Definitely! They are your parents, after all, Kiara. Take it from a guy who wishes he can talk to his dad one last time. I don't want you to regret anything."

What he said really struck a chord with me. He was right! I really didn't want to regret anything. And I really wanted to know why mom never actually visited me when she came to the rehab.

"You are right! I will give them a call later," I said, tearing off a big piece of the toast.

Raul looked happy at my realization and my appetite.

“Kiara! I was meaning to ask you...”

“Tell me!” I replied with my mouth still full of delicious toast

“Would you be interested in meeting my mom?”

I was taken aback by his sudden wish to make two of his worlds collide. Wait! Did he just ask me to meet his mom? This is huge. Is this too soon? This is getting really serious.

“Yes! Sure. Would love to,” I replied timorously.

CHAPTER 20

"Relax, Kiara! Today is going to be a good day." I kept chanting to myself as I got ready in front of the mirror. I looked back at the woman standing in front of me. It was a tiring year, but I can't believe she had survived that. And if she could survive that ...she could survive anything.

I can survive anything!

Affirmations were my thing. It's how I kept myself going through rehabilitation.

Within minutes after the much-needed pep talk, I was in front of Puzzles contemplating on all of my life choices that led me to this moment. As I stepped in, I heard a familiar voice shouting out my name -

"Kiara!"

I turned to find Rachel calling out to me from the corner booth.

Rachel! John's wife and ...Jake's cousin-sister!

It's been about two years since our last encounter, and she never looked prettier. I wouldn't say we were very close, but we did have mutual respect for each other. She never questioned me about my personal life, nor did I about hers. We kept it strictly about topics on weather and career.

"Heyyy! How have you been?" said Rachel jumping out of her seat and hugging me, "You know John, and I tried meeting you many times when you were in..."

"I know! John told me. I am good. How are things with you? I am sorry for not seeing you at that time. I was going through a very rough period, and I needed to be alone."

I observed her as she took the chair opposite of mine and glanced back at me with a smile; A coy smile. She definitely wanted something from me.

"I understand!" she said, looking at me with the same sympathetic expression I have been tired of getting ever since the rehab. "I actually called you to discuss something important."

There it was. Imaginary finger snaps were going around in my head.

Rachel proceeded to take a folder and placed it on the table with the brightest smile on her face. It was different this time. It wasn't coy but inviting.

"I think this is going to make you happy."

I slowly opened the pages to see a well-drafted contract. Bright red letters - NDTV stared back at me.

"I want you to be a talk show host on NDTV's digital platform! A weekly show with a special segment on literature. Your input can be valuable. If it picks up, it can be a daily thing on the channel. I pitched the idea, and the network is very interested. What do you think?"

A talk show host! Me! This was like a dream come true. An opportunity I never knew would ever cross my path. I look back at Rachel, baffled.

"Oh, My God! Rachel! This is ...This is big!"

I couldn't stop gushing over the unexpected twist in events. My hands were shaking at this point. I had to forcefully bite my cheek to get myself to calm down.

"I know! That's why I want you to take your time and think it through. But it would be great if you can let me know by next week."

"Rachel! Thank you ...I mean ...really! Thank you!"

She reached out for my hands, clasped in hers, and said,

"Kiara! You have been through so much. Whatever happened between you and Jake ...it's all old news …People don't remember that infamous TV moment anymore. As a matter of fact, the network believes that it will be a nice way to show your redemption. People do enjoy a good turned-around tale. Whether you accept it or not…your books still make a huge impact to this day. I really hope you say yes to this project."

Rachel was really good at selling, and I already felt sold. I panicked for a second, thinking about the last time I was on television. But she was right. I owed my readers an apology, and this definitely was a great way to start redemption.

"Thanks, Rachel! I am definitely going to think about it!" I nodded back to her in assurance.

"I am glad. And you came with a very high recommendation."

"Recommendation?"

"Yes! Sana! We work closely with her firm, and it was her idea!"

CHAPTER 21

My phone alarm rang with the reminder -

11:00 am - Therapy appointment

30 minutes to go.

I hurriedly tied up my shoes, grabbed the folder with all the storyline drafts left by Raul for me to proofread, and rushed to my Uber downstairs. Saturday morning never looked this busy. I sighed at the thought.

With one hand holding the Starbucks coffee cup and the other proofreading the drafts on my lap, I set out to seize the day, but alas, the universe had other plans, I suppose. My cab stopped mid-way due to a puncture, and no other Uber drivers were around. Nor a rickshaw. Just when I lost all hope and almost called Raul for help, a car slowed down in front of me and opened its windows.

"Kiara! My child! How are you, dear?"

It was Miss Rose! What a relief it was to see her kind and calming smile. Her face beamed with joy. A sight for sore eyes!

"Hop in! I can see you are having some car trouble. Please! Let me give you a ride!"

"Are you sure, Miss Rose?" I asked reluctantly though I very much didn't have another option.

She nodded in acknowledgment.

I jumped into the car and hugged her in sheer happiness. "Oh! Miss Rose! I missed you so much. Especially your tight hug!"

"Oh, child! You can always come and visit me at the rehabilitation center." she said, reciprocating the hug and signaling me to put on the seat belt, "Where are you off to?"

"To Saket!"

"To the mall?"

"To Therapy."

I looked over to Miss Rose to see her reaction to what I just said. Oddly enough, she seemed unfazed.

"Are you expecting me to say something, my child?"

She chuckled at my curiosity.

"Well, kind of ..." I replied with a hint of a smile.

"You had a hard year, Kiara! I am just glad that you are going to therapy. Now, where in Saket is it?"

Miss Rose did seem eager to change the topic and checked directions with me, to reach the clinic instead. I didn't want to make her feel uncomfortable either. Soon enough, we were at the entrance of the clinic, and just before I stepped out, something itched me to ask her,

"Miss Rose! If I ask you something...will you be honest with me?"

"What is it, child?"

"Did Mom visit me in rehab?"

She looked down and answered in a condescending tone,

"Yes!"

I gave out a deep sigh; Not the kind you would give out of surprise, but more of an agitated one. I was hoping to hear the opposite, and Miss Rose's silent confession had begun to throw me to the edge.

"Why didn't you tell me?"

"Because she didn't want me to. She cares about you, Kiara! She is still your mother..."

"Yeah! Thanks, Miss Rose!"

I stepped out of the car in frustration and headed to the clinic.

Why would mom come all the way to rehab and not visit me?

Why did she come all alone?

Where was Dad?

Why did the clinic keep it a secret?

My mind was all over the place, and my heart had begun to beat faster in the chest. I could slowly feel a knot form in the pit of my stomach, body wavering out of the sudden revelation and lungs gasping for copious amounts of air.

I had a mild panic attack.

CHAPTER 22

"What is it? Why are you so agitated?"

"Nothing! I can't find those earrings! That's all!"

I screamed at the top of my lungs as I searched under the cupboard.

It wasn't NOTHING! I was freaking out. Meeting parents was a big deal for me, and it didn't go well in the past with Jake's parents either. It was like deja vu all over again.

What if Raul's mom hated me?

Is it even advisable to meet parents this early in a relationship?

Technically we have been together for over months ...almost a year!

Do I really need to put up a facade again?

I finally got hold of the missing pair and proceeded to lock it on my ear while looking at the petrified girl standing in front of me in the mirror. Raul paused, at first, before slowly putting his hands around my waist from behind and slowly kissed my neck. My body shuddered to his touch.

"Let's not go!"

"What?!"

I turned around and looked back at him, confused. He calmly locked eyes with mine and lingered. Too calm, in fact.

"You are not comfortable. And I don't want to pressure you into doing anything you are not comfortable with. Just remember …you can tell me anything! But be honest with me …that's all I want."

He said, kissing my lips and holding me tighter. His warm body eased mine and paced my breathing.

Raul never ceases to amaze me. He could always read my mind without having to go through all the drama, which usually went behind the scenes with Jake. Raul was different. He was attentive, calm, composed, and I really really really ...loved him.

I love him!

That's the first time I felt that for any guy.

"I love you."

My lips gave it away without my knowing. Raul looked back at me with that sparkle in his eyes and kissed me even harder. The sudden confession seemed to spark something in him, and he smiled through the labyrinth of kisses. He held me back again beamed,

"I love you too."

This! This was what the word "love" felt like. I could get used to this. But I had to come clean to him about everything …about Jake, Sana, the wedding …everything.

As the voices in my head went through a hurricane of emotions, Raul interrupted,

"I love you too, Kiara!" his expression dropped, and his voice deepened, "But we need to talk!"

Chapter 23

"Miss Kiara! Are you ready? ...Miss? Uhhh…Miss?"

I was snapped back to reality by the voice of a perturbed assistant who was constantly asking me to change positions to avoid headspace in the viewfinder. The NDTV office was nothing like I had imagined. It was quite huge with bright lights and their signature red lining, from the logo along the background that added the much-needed clean-cut persona of the brand.

Rachel stood at the corner with her crew giving them instructions on how to go about with the segment while the rest of the NDTV team kept bustling in and out of the room with scripts and adjusting the lights to soften the frame.

Everything about this looked like a scene from *The Newsroom,* except it was nothing like that. I was just another washed-out author trying to make books sound cool again with my weekly jargon.

"Okay! Everything looks good here. Let's take ten, everyone. Coffee and snacks are available downstairs. Don't forget to show your staff ID to avail it!"

Rachel screamed from her corner, gave me a nod, and proceeded to join her crew for coffee downstairs. I sighed in relief and slowly occupied the lonely table overlooking the metro rail and the heavy traffic near the signal. They all looked like ants scurrying to reach their ant holes, a thought so stupid I couldn't help but chuckle. The scent of freshly baked cookies and coffee was slowly filling up the room as the crew slowly returned with their half-brim cups. Some of them had grouped outside the building for a smoke. So I was definite that it would take more than just ten minutes for the crew to be whole again.

I looked down at the open text message on my phone -

"I am sorry. I should have told you sooner."

The message from Raul was vague and honestly, confusing. Events that transpired last night began flooding back into my mind-

"What is it, Raul? Is everything fine?"

I asked with concern as I tugged along the hem of his tee. His head was bowed down in confusion and disgust.

"I don't know how to say this …and honestly I have been struggling with it. I should have said this earlier …or the minute it happened."

At this point, Raul was pacing back and forth in the apartment. A triggered Muffy followed him around as if he shared his feeling of restlessness.

"What is it?"

"It's not a big deal. Maybe it is …I don't know. Just know that I love you, and you love me. Hold on to that, okay? Hold on to that thought when I say this …"

He clasped both of my hands in his and directed my eyes to his. His eyes, once bright hazel, were now dim with darkness. There were tears at the corners begging to be let out.

"Last week, when you had gone to meet Rachel, I had gone to my previous literary agent's office for a small task."

"Yes, you had told me that." I tried to fasten the conversation. My heart hangs on to his every word.

"Well, I ran into Rose there. We started talking, and it felt just like old times...and one thing led to another and…"

"And?!" my tone now louder than usual …

"And she kissed me."

I felt my heart drop, "What?!"

"She kissed me! I didn't kiss back. I immediately drew away from her!"

"Why didn't you tell me sooner?"

"Because…I love you, and I didn't want to hurt you."

"No!" I sat on the couch in disbelief, "No! You would have been honest if you loved me. No ...no…"

There goes that expression "turning tables" in a matter of minutes. Love was a dangerous word, indeed. The man I loved now stood before me like a stranger.

"Please leave!"

With tears streaming down my cheeks, I quickly opened the front door and directed him to leave the apartment. We were both crying. Eyes red with pain, skin sore from the exhaustion, and lips trembling from all the words that had just been let out. Raul gathered his jacket and his phone. Before passing me by, he paused for a second to look into my eyes -

"I really do love you. I fucked up!"

"You did!" I sniffled in anger …in pain …in love.

This must be what Karma feels like…I chanted to myself when Raul spoke again,

"I know I fucked up …but I ain't giving up on you."

Chapter 24

"And cut! That's a wrap, everyone!"

The director had called for pack up, and the crew began to scurry around again.

It was my last day at the studio. At least for a while.

The first season of my online segment had come to an end. Truth be told, it was everything I had imagined working in a production house to be and more. And it also served as solace from all the dire things happening in reality. Every time my heels touched the studio I was a whole new person - a charming quirky author giving my take on the upcoming books, sharing my two cents on the films made from books, and interviewing the bestsellers from different fields. In the span of three months, I had met more people than I ever did in the last 2 years. My social battery was slowly getting back to the way it used to be, but this time it was different.

Different 'cause I remained sober through it all. Despite everything going on, I was sober.

A fact even I was appalled by.

Raul and I remained in touch for the past three months but only via email. We were still working on the book, and it felt like all the chapters were coming to an end - real and reel.

The first month was the hardest post-break-up. I cried myself to sleep the first week because I believed I wasn't capable of love. Almost bought myself a beer in the second week to ease the pain, but I decided to throw myself into work to turn off my emotions instead. The third week was the hardest as I kept missing Raul every second. He occasionally texted me saying how we deserved a second shot which usually ended up in us fighting. By the fourth week, we decided to communicate strictly via email and talk only about the book to ensure the completion of our tasks. There was too much at stake!

I sat at my desk at home, segregating the stack of papers beside me, and let out a deep sigh when I realized how the show and the book wrapped up at the same time. I was going to miss the process of them both. When I had first left the rehabilitation center, I was clueless about what my future held. Fast forward here I was with stacks of paper on my desk; One was a pile of show script, and the other contained the fair draft of the book.

My phone suddenly beeped with a message from Raul -

Hey! Free this Friday night? I want to take you out for dinner. Consider it a celebratory one for having finished the book. Please! I want to see you.

The last line made my heart skip a beat. I wanted to see him too. I missed him; his smile, his eyes, his scent, his lips.

Oh! His lips.

His lips that had kissed another.

“I need more time, Raul.”

Message sent.

I collapsed on the couch next to Muffy. He slowly advanced forward for cuddles.

“You are the only man I need in my life, Muffy.” I gave him a playful kiss on the forehead, and he immediately reciprocated with a lick on my cheeks.

The phone beeped again. Expecting a response from Raul, I picked it up but was immediately dumbfounded by what I found. A text from John with a link to a news article -

“Actor Jake and Chef Rina have reportedly been dating for 5 months.”

CHAPTER 25

I had the weekend all to myself.

No manuscript deadlines.

No practicing scripts.

Nothing.

Just me in my pajamas with Muffy huddled up near the corner window. A warm cup of coffee rested on one hand while my phone on the other. I re-read the tabloid headlines again in the "Entertainment" section -

"Actor Jake and Chef Rina have reportedly been dating for 5 months."

The supposed romance sparked between the two on the sets of their new TV show scheduled to debut later this spring. The happy couple confirmed their dating rumors through their respective PR teams later this evening."

5 months! She was dating my ex-fiancé for a whole of 5 months, and she never once mentioned it during our series of endless FaceTime.

"So what's up with you? How is the shoot going?" I would constantly check up on her and call her on her breaks between schedules.

"Good. Same old same old. Forget about me. Tell me about Raul! How is it going?" she replied nonchalantly. Almost as if she was desperately trying to change the subject.

"Good. Actually better than good. Great! I don't know. I am just happy. He makes me happy. I think I love him, Rina!"

Rina's face lit up almost immediately from the revelation.

"Kiara! You are in love! I can't believe it! Ah! I am so excited and happy and ah! Kiara …this makes me so happy."

She exclaimed in happiness. A conversation I had with her about four days before my confession to Raul.

Now that I think about it, her conversations did start to sound vague.

"Kiara! Have you ever been in a situation where you had to choose between two important things in your life?"

"Kiara! Should someone actually be honest even if it means losing on something great?"

"Kiara! What's more important - honesty or passion?"

And all this while I thought she was talking about her career. Little did I know she was battling a war in her head about being honest with me.

But she should have been honest. Was a boy more important than your own best friend?

I paused for a minute as what I had just thought slowly began to sink in.

Was a boy more important than your own best-friend?

Did a fake relationship with Jake really matter more to me than Sana?

This was *Karma,* after all. Tears began to well up in the corner of my eye-lids.

I have finally come undone.

Sniffling hard, I collapsed on the couch and for the first time in a very, very, very long time …

I cried.

I wailed.

I screamed.

I panted, trying to take in the air between the muffled cries.

Poor Muffy kept wailing alongside me while licking my salty tears and trying to comfort me in the only way he knew how.

When I finally got myself to calm down, I hurriedly ordered an Uber to Noida.

It was time to face my past. It was time to face Sana.

Chapter 26

"Kiara! Tell me!

Tell me! Dammit!

Are you okay? Please tell me …

I am coming now!"

I tried to fight back the tears that were streaming down my blood-stained cheeks but in vain.

"Okay," I muttered in pain back to Raul on the phone.

There was shattered glass all over my hair and open wounds and scabs on my arms from the same. My watch with a broken frame showed the time to be exactly 6 pm. It was late March which meant winters hadn't left Delhi completely yet, and the sun set even before it struck 6.

My Uber had crashed into a food truck while speeding along the Noida highway.

The food truck managed to hit and run unscathed. But the Uber had lost its balance and crashed into the nearby lamp post. It took a few minutes, but a few good people managed to pull my Uber driver and me. The driver had hit his forehead in the steering wheel, causing him to instantly blackout from the collision.

I, on the other hand, was the first one to come to consciousness.

"I can't believe she survived that crash!"

"She is really lucky to have survived!"

I overheard some aunties talk to each other as I got placed inside the ambulance in a stretcher.

Within a few minutes, I was at the emergency ward, where a nurse had begun to treat the scratches and scabs with an antiseptic. A female doctor with a nametag Maria stood next to her observing my swollen shoulder over the semi-torn t-shirt.

"Is the Uber driver alright?"

The nurse nodded at my concerned question.

"Yes, he sprained his neck, but he will be fine soon. He got saved by the airbag. You, on the other hand, have a fractured shoulder, cuts on your arms, legs, and forehead."

I listened to Doctor Maria half attentively. It was as if half my brain had become numb. The nurse seemed to have noticed and exclaimed,

"I am going to get this all bandaged and then treat your shoulder next. Alright?"

I shook my head in approval. The doctor whispered some details to the nurse while pointing out my wounds and directing her fingers to the scribbles she had made on her doctor pad. She then looked at me, nodded with a smile, and exited my territory to head to the next patient in an emergency.

The nurse took out rolls of cotton and began to prepare a solution to be added to my shoulder before casting it up.

"Have you contacted your next of kin? Will he or she be here soon?"

Before I could reply to the nurse, a voice interjected,

"Yes! It's me! I am here!"

Raul stood before me, drenched in his own sweat and barely breathing. He held a helmet in one hand and the keys to a bike in the other. He seemed to have driven a motorbike to reach here quicker. His eyes were sullen with shock, anger and sadness. He quickly placed the helmet on the table beside me, keys in his pocket, and proceeded towards me.

But before he could even touch me, I sprung on to him. My shoulders seared with pain but his familiar touch eased the ache. His musky scent enveloped me as I buried myself on his chest, staining his jacket with my blood and tears.

He was quick to embrace me in his cold yet warm hands and kissed my head to calm me down.

"Baby, it's okay! I am here."

At least for now …it's going to be okay. He is here!

CHAPTER 27

I woke up with a startle. My breath hitched in my throat when I realized Raul's warm breath in the nape of my neck and his arms around my waist. He was curled up next to me in the hospital bed.

I slowly turned my head to the other side to avoid waking him up.

2:00 AM

The blue light from the digital clock filled the small space on the bedside table. I was moved to a private room about a few hours back, and Raul insisted on staying.

"I am not leaving you alone. You are getting discharged tomorrow anyway. Let me take you home," Raul said as he clasped my hands. "A friend will drop my car at the hospital in the morning and take back the motorbike. I will drive you home."

I didn't argue ...I didn't want to argue at all. I just wanted to stay by his side. He looked the most beautiful when he was asleep. A sense of calm enveloped the atmosphere around me as I watched him slowly twitch from movements and proceed to snuggle me harder.

“Are you awake, baby?” his hoarse sleepy voice cut through the air, “Do you want me to get you something?”

He could barely open his eyes.

I shook my head and turned around to pull him toward my embrace. He moved swiftly towards me while being careful not to disturb my shoulder, buried his face into my chest, and kissed my neck faintly. He paused for a second, breathed my scent in, and trailed the kisses till he reached my lips. Softly pressed his lips on mine and pulled me in. Our tongues were fighting for dominance, and our bodies withered from each other’s touch.

“I missed you,”

He breathed into the kiss.

“I missed you so damn much, Kiara.”

A tear escaped from the corner of my eye. I was vulnerable, but vulnerability never felt like weakness in front of him. It felt more like coming home and being safe.

“I am really sorry. All I know is that I love you and I can’t …I can’t be like this … I can’t be without you,”

He broke the kiss and hugged me harder. I rested my head on his. I could stay like this forever.

“Raul?”

"Yes, baby!"

His hazel eyes opened swiftly and interlocked with mine. His eyebrows furrowed into his forehead, slightly confused by my low tone yet wildly attractive.

"I still love you too."

I whispered down my breath as he began to shower me with excited kisses all over my face.

"There is no going back from this! You know that, right?"

He smirked and continued to shower me with more.

I nodded and smiled through them all.

As I savored every moment, my phone suddenly beeped with a message. It was a response to something I had sent months ago.

K. Let's meet.

- Sana.

CHAPTER 28

The last I spoke to Sana in person was about 2 years ago. Right before my epic meltdown on national television. News 18 had scheduled an interview with me about my much-talked-about engagement with the renowned Jake Matthews. I, on the other hand, was eagerly looking forward to it to plug the launch of my second book at the time.

The Power Couple!

We were deemed by all the publications and channels as the fake relationship got a lot of attention. Our careers had peaked after the dating rumors and the launch of my first book; Jake's, Sana's, and mine.

Sana's agency was proclaimed as the production house of talents, thanks to my book rising the bestseller chart and Jake's first role as a supporting actor in a film that broke the box office and charmed the audience. Soon she was signing in more talents, and her small team was beginning to get bigger by the week.

But Sana wasn't herself anymore. She rarely smiled, and when she did, it was an impassive one that let others think she was completely on board with everything happening around her.

“Sana, I never thought he would actually fall for me! Believe me! I …”

I desperately tried to find the words to comfort her a few months before the engagement. Jake had broken up with her two months into our fake relationship on the pretext that he had fallen head over heels for me and that whatever they had was just a fling. He assured her that it was never in his best intention to hurt her and that she and he were never a match in the first place. The aftermath was a drunk Sana at the doorstep of my parents’ house where I was residing at the time, drunkenly swearing about how I, her best friend, and the only one she ever trusted, ruined her life with my selfishness.

“You got everything you want!”

She sniffled through her cries, picked herself from my bedroom floor, and threw herself on my bed, “You used me to get your name up, used my boyfriend, got yourself all the fame and attention, and what did I get? Nothing. Nada! Zilch.”

I sat by her side and tried to get her to drink some coffee my mom had made to sober her up. She refused and continued to wail more in my direction,

“I loved him, Kiara! I still love him! And you took him away from me!”

“Sana …please listen to me ...I ...”

Suddenly she sat upright as if something had snapped inside her. She wiped the remaining tears off her swollen cheeks, proceeded to look at herself in my vanity mirror, checked her eyes, and sullenly replied,

"I have seen the way you look at him. I always thought you did it cause he was handsome. But a part of me knew you liked him too. Not love. But definitely infatuation."

"Sana, please …"

"It's fine, Kiara. You like him. He loves you. You guys are already in a relationship in everyone's eye. Let's not call it fake anymore." she said, straightening up the dress she was wearing while avoiding any eye contact with me and constantly gazing at her drunken state in the mirror.

"Sana, please stop," I pleaded, but the way her eyes glared right back reassured me that things are never going to be the same again.

"I am going to close this as one bad chapter I had to learn life lessons from. And Kiara …"

"Yeah?"

"You have one month to find yourself another publicist. My team will take care of you until then. I, on the other hand, would never like to see you or talk to you again."

She spoke sternly, took one look at my eyes welled up with tears trying to make sense of everything, her eyes emotionless and sunk in from all the crying and left the house. It was the last we saw of or spoke to each other.

CHAPTER 29

"So you heard?" asked John as he added two teaspoons of sugar to his espresso. He stirred the mixture frantically for a minute and proceeded to order two spinach quiche to the table. Months looked like years on him. His beard had grown uneven with shades of grey and black. His hair unkept, and his eyes demanding sleep.

"It's like Deja vu! Except for its Rina's name there now instead of yours."

I breathed a long sigh that instantly caught his attention.

"I haven't talked to Rina yet. I did leave her a couple of messages, but they didn't get delivered. I am pretty sure she changed her number to avoid interviewers hitting her up. Been there, so I understand."

John seemed to be surprised by how lethargic I was about the whole situation. He cocked an eyebrow in confoundment.

"So you are okay with all this? Your best friend is dating your ex-fiancé! You are really okay?"

I shrugged and fell back on the chair and attempted to add another spoon of sugar to the coffee just like John did, but immediately stopped myself when I realized how absent-minded I was at this point. I was unknowingly mimicking things. Maybe I was not okay. Maybe I am. I was still trying to figure it out.

"Sana replied to my message from months ago. We are meeting next week." I spoke apathetically.

"Wow. The way you guys left things …I never expected you guys to rekindle your friendship." John said unambiguously.

"I wouldn't say rekindling, but it's the first step to something. She had suggested my name for the talk show to Rachel. Seems like Rachel and she are on really good terms due to work. Good for them." I said as I stared at the window. Delhi summers were slowly beginning, and the weather outside had started to get hot. A part of my brain began to imagine how great it would be to go horse-riding with

Raul a few more times before the weather gets unbearable. The thought made me smile. A bright and noticeable one.

"I haven't seen that smile in so long. A broken shoulder with a cast. Yet this is the happiest I have ever seen you." John said admiringly as I glanced back at him while keeping my smile intact,

"Rachel told me about this new character in your life called Raul. Ghostwriter, right?"

I nodded in excitement.

"Is he treating you right?"

I blushed and nodded again. He was right. This was probably the happiest I have ever been. As I got lost in my happy thoughts, John interrupted reluctantly,

"Kiddo! There is something I wanted to discuss with you."

There was a sudden change in the mood of the room. His eyes dropped down as if he was unwilling to speak the next couple of sentences. He kept fidgeting until he finally found the words to say,

"You know I have been searching for investors for my new business. I recently ran into your parents, and they decided to partner with my company."

"That's great. They always liked you anyway. They were terrible parents but brilliant entrepreneurs. I hope it works out for you." I replied half-excitedly. Part of me wondered if they ever talked about me together, about my whereabouts, about my accident. It was too much to ask of them, yet too little even though they practically shunned me out of their lives. They were always close to John and his parents. So this definitely didn't come as a surprise. It was just a matter of time.

"I know you don't talk to your parents anymore," John proceeded to speak in the same perturbed tone, "but there is something I think you should know. It's about your Dad."

My heart dropped as he spoke, and my mind began to read way too much between the lines.

"What?!"

CHAPTER 30

I was standing outside Puzzles, rapidly pacing while waiting for Raul to reach the cafe. John's revelation was pushing me to the edge, and I wanted answers.

"Your Dad was found to have arrhythmia and had undergone surgery for the same."

My eyes widened, and I could hear my own heart skip a beat as he uttered the words.

"He was in the hospital for a while and in a treatment center right after that for recovery. Turns out he was in Fortis center, which was quite near to the rehabilitation center you stayed in."

Everything was slowly making sense - Mom's unannounced visit, Miss Nancy figuring it out on the records, and Miss Rose's reluctance to share any further information on the matter because she must have thought it wasn't her place to share, or maybe my mother didn't want me to know. Why wouldn't they want me to know of something as important and big as this?

"But I don't get it. Why didn't anyone bloody tell me about this?!"

My voice had begun to crack, and John was quick to give me a glass of water to calm me down.

"Drink this first!"

I quickly gulped it down and signaled for seconds.

"I don't think your parents intended to let me know either. But your dad wanted to be honest before any business transaction. I also think he might have perhaps hidden it from you to make sure you wouldn't relapse when you were trying so hard to get over your addiction."

He said, filling up my glass to the brim.

I downed it immediately and mumbled,

"Perhaps!"

After John had left for a meeting, I took a few minutes to ponder over everything and convinced myself to meet my parents. But I didn't want to do it alone. Not like this. With a broken shoulder and bruised body.

"I would like to join you if you don't mind," Raul spoke in a honeyed tone over the phone. "I know it's not the ideal way to meet your parents ...but …they would be at ease to know there is someone by your side especially, in the state you are in."

Agreed. Raul's chirpy personality would soften the blow and also reassure them of her well-being. We have been estranged, but they were still my parents.

CHAPTER 31

"Kiara!"

My mom's voice that once screamed my name out in assertiveness now sounded mellow and quiet feeble. Her skin wrinkled and worn out from the years but her eyes still shone as bright as how I remembered her from my childhood - kind and calming.

"How have you been? And who is your friend here?"

She instructed the maid to keep the two cups of coffee in front of us. Raul was quick to beam back at my mom with his brightest smile and introduce himself,

"Namaste aunty! I am Raul. Kiara's ghostwriter."

"Oh! You must be working on her new book. Nice to meet you beta", mom replied with a warm smile and turned towards me with as if she needed my assurance to believe him

"He is my boyfriend"

I said in a low tone under my breath and proceeded to take a sip of the coffee. Mom seemed to study my behavior like she always did. She paused and smiled reassuringly at Raul,

"That's nice. My Kiara is a handful. Hope she is not troubling you."

I scoffed at her remark and gazed at her unbothered self. Mom had skillfully mastered the art of pretending like everything was fine while downplaying the intensity of any situation to work it according to her favor. But some games were too old for me and I didn't want in on it anymore.

"You say as if all I ever did was trouble you"

The color from her face began to fade away slowly.

"Why didn't you tell me? And where is Dad?"

My impatience was getting the better of my agitated tone and it didn't sit well with mom. She seemed to have been taken aback from the sudden accusation. Raul slowly brushed my back signaling me to watch my tone and words

"He is sleeping upstairs. He takes his nap during this time. Do you want to wait or do you want to come another time?", mom's assertive tone was back.

"I will stay"

Mom nodded as I placed the coffee mug back on the table, "Okay. You can wait here or in your room.

We haven't changed anything. It's still as it is. I am heading out for a bit as I had to get some medicines for your Dad. I am just going to order the Uber and…"

"Let me take you aunty! I have got my car.", Raul interrupted and quickly jumped to the chance to help her out.

"It's okay beta! It's quite far. You can wait here with…"

"Please aunty! I insist!"

Another one bites the dust.

I thought to myself as mom slowly gave into Raul's charms. Soon they were out of the house and on their way to the pharmacy.

With a little time to kill on my hands I decided to go back to my room that was forgotten in a corner of this house for two and a half years. The flight of stairs leading to my room though well kept now looked shabby and weather trodden. I slowly turned the door knob to a familiar yet forlorn room with floors that creak at every step and the small window in the far corner let very little sunlight to illuminate the room. A large wooden bookcase laid on the right corner with an array of books covered with a coat of dust. The bed on the other corner with a floral bed sheet over it. The posters of Harry Potter still hung on the walls alongside some newspaper cuttings of reviews of my first book with a frame around it. I stepped beside my wardrobe with a thin rectangular floor mirror. The woman in the mirror was no more the angsty teenager with a dream and dire need to please everyone and do anything to get her way. She was now a calm, composed and beautiful woman in her 20's who believed in herself and most of all wise enough to accept and embrace her flaws. A smile played in one corner of my lips. The walls of that room had seen so many versions of her over the years. But this version of her.... the happy one ... was my favorite.

CHAPTER 32

"Papa! Are you comfortable now?", I asked as I neatly tucked the sides of his blanket under the bed. Dad, who once stood tall with his heavy shoulder hanging from his widened frame, now laid before me curled up on the bed.

"I am okay now!", he said nestling himself better and placing one hand on mine.

The veins on his hand stood out extra from his worn out skin. Age was making a mark on his dull face and it was beginning to make my heart heavy to look at him this way.

" Are you taking your tablets properly? Getting your checkups done regularly?", I asked frantically to which my tired Dad replied, "Yes! How have you been?"

I was caught off guard from something as simple as the line "How have you been!?" from my Dad's feeble mouth. Tears welled up from the corner of my eyes and within seconds my face buried in his lap while gasping for breath between the wailing.

I had missed his voice.

I had missed this feeling of endearment.

And more than ever I had missed him.

Nothing ever good comes with waging war with the ones you love. There is no win or lose in this complicated warfare. You lose either ways when it's your parents on the other end of the battlefield.

"You should have told me! I should have been there for you.",

I mumbled between my sniffled cries.

Dad patted my head and beamed back at me with the most widest smile

"You are now!"

All was well.

CHAPTER 33

"What did you guys talk about?"

I asked inquisitively at an overly excited Raul behind the steering wheel. He was insanely happy after the short trip he had with my mom.

"This one is a keeper", mom had whispered to my ear as I hugged her goodbye. Dad seemed to have taken a liking for this 6 feet man as well.

"I like you boy. Please come by more often and give this old man your time of day.", Dad had requested when we bid farewell after the long yet eventful day.

Raul was now driving us back in glee with this happy grin plastered on the face and I couldn't help but feel a little giddy with happiness myself.

"Tell me! Did she mention about my weird childhood habits or something?"

"Like the time you wet the bed"

I looked back at Raul with the most flustered and horror stricken face to which he chuckled and said,

"Wait? Did you really? Haha I was just playing with you"

Raul was uncontrollably laughing and I was made. He opened the car's sunroof and let in some light and fresh air. The car was glistening under the sun, metal soaking up the warm rays and his face practically glowing from the golden hour and I couldn't help but appreciate this beautiful man right before me. Absolutely freaking beautiful- inside out.

How did I get this lucky?

On a whim I leaned over to his side with his skin just a few inches away from mine, breathed in his intoxicating scent and felt it travel all throughout my body, slowly held his chin with my left hand and planted soft yet deep kisses on his left cheek.

It was his turn to smile through it all. And smile he did. A gorgeous one at that.

CHAPTER 34

I absentmindedly searched the apartment for my house keys while being fully aware of the fact that it's actually dangling right on the door frame. I had spent the whole morning cleaning up as a way to evade my mind from fully going bizarre thinking of the events set to happen later that night.

"Are you sure you don't want me to give you a ride? I can drop you to Gurgaon and pick you up a bit later. I had some work there anyway", Raul had insisted on our drive back from my parents.

"What kind of work?", I had asked inquisitively. It was a rarity to watch Raul not mention details. He was the type who would even mention the number of sugar cubes he put in his coffee. An annoying habit for some but an adorable one for me. That's why seeing him put off the subject matter was seeming unusual for the conversation. He noticed my furrowed eyebrows and was quick to disperse my unwanted collected thoughts.

"It's the final paperwork for the ranch."

His face dropped at his confession. It was pretty evident that he was totally against the idea of selling. It was the last of what he had left that belonged to his Dad. But tough times call for tough measures. He shook his head as if he was involuntarily trying to shake his feelings away from his body.

"Ah! Well that's that. So like I was saying… let me drop you. I will pick you on the way back. I think an hour and a half would suffice right? To meet Sana?"

I nodded in approval. It was going to be a long emotional evening. For both of us.

The roads leading to the gurgaon highway were jam packed with vehicles and pedestrians alike. Friday evenings were usually the busiest for this town and the road seems to be the evidence of that.

"We will reach in another 40 minutes I suppose", Raul said honking the car horn harder at the car before us before swiftly turning towards me, "Nervous hun?"

I shook my head in dismay.

"I know it's not my place… but… We have 40 minutes to kill and now would be a good time. Don't you think? Do you mind telling me what actually went wrong between you, Jake and Sana?"

Here it was. The long dreaded moment I have been cautiously dodging all this while. I looked into Raul's eyes that gazed back at me with a dire need to console me irrespective of what I was going to say. He truly had a way of making me feel like everything was going to be fine.

So I slowly opened my Pandora box filled with betrayal, recklessness and the series of bad choices. Raul listened to it silently for the next 30 minutes, briefly nodding to the important moments and dropping a "hmm" to show his acknowledgement. Part of me wanted to halt in between and assure him that I wasn't the same heartless girl anymore and part of me wanted to see how he would reciprocate after knowing all my demons. By the end of it I feared he might begin seeing me in a whole different light but he just sat there staring at the lights in front of him as he cautiously drove us both through the crusty roads. A brief silence till the destination.

We were soon at sector 29 - the most happening bar street of Gurgaon. As I struggled to slowly wear my heels to get off the car Raul's hand was quick to grab by chin and draw it closer to his. His fingers traced the hair near my cheeks and slowly placed it behind my ear. He moved in closer, placed a warm kiss on my lips and whispered under his breath,

"I love you. So damn much. And nothing will ever change that!"

CHAPTER 35

There was a skip in my steps towards the bar I was supposed to meet Sana. A happy grin could be seen plastered on my face unintentionally and I just couldn't stop. I stepped into the elevator to head towards the bar area from the lobby and slowly began grazing my fingers to recall what had just happened a few minutes back. My cheeks stained pink from the aftermath.

Soon enough I was at the crowded bar and on mentioning Sana's name the waitress slowly ushered me to a corner booth. The bar was Sana's client as well so the treatment was indeed royalty. What I was most surprised about was how visiting bars never bothered me anymore. There was no temptation and I was proud of myself.

I ordered myself a virgin Bloody Mary and waited patiently for her. After about 15 minutes a tall brunette in a small black dress that seemed fit for the evening slowly approached the booth. Sana had never looked this prettier.

She had a warming smile unlike the cold alter ego I had imagined in my head all this while. Her skin was glowing and her hair looked like a black cascade of waterfall. Her loud red lip shade complimented her look. She definitely still was a head-turner.

"How have you been?", she gleamed as she nestled herself opposite to my table, "You look pretty good for someone who was just out of rehab last year"

She winked and proceeded to order a Bloody Mary for herself as well, a dirty one.

"I have been good. And...how about you?", a slight stutter gave away my anxiousness. I was really finding it hard to hold a conversation and realized it was just going to get harder if I didn't cut to the chase immediately. So I took a deep breath and uttered,

"Sana! I am sorry! For … for everything! I missed you! I missed my best friend"

Sana gazed empathetically back at me on hearing my sudden outburst. And I could see it clearly that she felt the same.

"Oh come here!"

She pranced off her seat and dragged me along with her. She hugged me in a tight grip and muttered in my ears, "I missed you too Kiara. I am sorry too. Let's let bygones be bygones."

I guess all we ever needed was some time.

The rest of the evening was spent catching up to all the years we had missed out on each other. Jake's name came up a few times amid our conversations but Sana seemed unfazed by it now. I later realized the reason when a bright diamond ring stared back at me from her ring finger. She was now happily engaged to one of the renowned reporters of NDTV named Tarun Roy. That explained the whole connection and circumstances that led to her recommending me for their digital venture.

"I recently met Natasha in the NDTV building when I was on my way to meet Tarun for lunch. She filled me in on everything and the possibility of a chance of season 2. I hope it works out", she said gobbling a load of crusted corn into her mouth, "She also spoke to me about your man. The ghost writer who worked on your latest book. How is it going? I would like to meet him soon."

She washed it down with a gulp of her second round of bloody mary. I watched her amusingly recollecting our previous drunken nights. It didn't seem like a gap of 2 and a half years at all.

"Yes! It's going great. I can't wait for you to meet him either. Our book is set to launch next month. He is just....amazing!"

"Seeing you in love was something I never thought I would be witnessing. Now that I am .... I can 100% say you are worse than a teenager who just discovered her first crush.", she chuckled

"Staaapphhhh", I reverted with a slight nudge on her shoulders.

It felt like old times.

CHAPTER 36

"I am glad you enjoyed the evening and I am glad you guys talked it out", Raul said as he drove us back to my apartment. I smiled back at him in happiness and questioned the events of his evening as well. He seemed quite happy unlike a broody and sad Raul I had imagined.

"Truth be told, something unexpected happened!", he said excitedly, " Turns out the buyer was an old friend of Dad's and he proposed an idea to me about a partnership in starting a bookstore cum cafe in that space."

"Raul! That's amazing! Are you going to do it?", I beamed back in excitement as well.

"I think so. In this way I would have solid income coming in, it's something I love and I will also have time on my hands working on my own book.", I stared back in awe by the words he just uttered unknowingly.

"Did you just say your 'own' book? Did I hear that right?"

I was overjoyed at this point and it seemed contagious cause Raul couldn't stop getting overwhelmed as well. He hurriedly nodded in assurance and I was quick to commemorate the happy moment with a kiss.

We reached downstairs of my apartment where we bid farewell. Raul didn't take up my invite to stay over as he had a long day driving around and he was definitely looking to hit the sack soon.

"You won't let me sleep and I won't be able to either with you lying right next to me", he chuckled and winked quite seductively, "Goodnight love!"

There definitely was some truth to that. I bit my lip as I thought about it as well.

I watched him drive away and slowly paced myself to my apartment. I was tired too and could actually use some sleep myself.

The door knob made a clicking sound to unlock and before I could head straight in I heard a voice call out my name from behind me in a feeble manner.

I turned around in curiosity only to find a tired and worn out looking Rina standing out in my hallway with three giant luggages behind her, each stamped by the French Airlines.

CHAPTER 37

The tea pot began to whistle and the sound was piercing through the tension in the room. I had invited Rina in for a cup of tea and to talk things over. She sat on the couch with her head down and occasionally took a peek at her watch. Her clothes and luggages seemed to give the notion that she had headed straight from the airport to my home.

"Rina! Did you go home?", I finally decided to break the ice, "It's late!"

Clearly we both had a long day. But Rina was adamant to stay put and speak things out. The only problem being there was no actual 'speaking'. She sniffled and cried for a few minutes, dabbed her eyes with the handkerchief and cried into it some more.

"I don't know what happened okay! This was never meant to happen...you know I wouldn't intentionally hurt you right. I hated him ...you know I hated him"

Rina was practically pacing to and fro from the corners of my apartment at this point. I sat on the couch watching her with my half cold cup of tea trying to put two and two together.

"I know. But why didn't you just tell me? Why did you avoid my calls and messages?"

"Because I was scared okay. And an idiot! And I am sorry Very sorry for being a terrible friend!", she said, throwing her hand in the air and finally collapsing right beside me. I slowly observed my friend who was now gasping for air between muffled cries. Her hair was messy and her eyes red from the constant crying. Her skin seemed weather beaten and her lips quivering from all the stress.

"Do you love him?", I asked while forcefully placing her head on my shoulders. She seemed to be taken aback from my gesture at first but slowly eased her worrisome head on mine.

"I do. I really do.", she sniffled some more.

"Then there is nothing to be sorry about. I am genuinely happy for you!", I said slowly patting her messy head with affection.

It wasn't just a say. I genuinely was happy for her. It didn't really matter to me anymore and I knew why. So did she.

"You know I am happy for you too!", she said sitting upright and wiping her tears away, " Sana told me all about it!"

"You guys spoke?", I asked, bewildered to which Rina immediately nodded.

Rina stayed over that night. Turned out she had an early morning flight to Melbourne as she was going to meet Jake at the set of his new movie shoot. She spent the entire night gushing over how they went from being frenemies to actually falling head over heels, how the show broke their expected view targets and the possibility of her permanently setting up her base in Paris. Things were looking great for her and I was immensely proud.

As she geared up to head out the door to catch her 5 am flight to Australia, I couldn't help but question her intentions in taking a pit stop in Delhi just for a mere 6 hours when she could have comfortably flown directly. To my surprise Rina said,

"Because Raul asked me to. He saw the tabloids and reached out to me a few weeks back. He was really concerned about you, about us! You got yourself a good one Kiara!"

I sure did.

CHAPTER 38

A year later.

"And cut! Let's take 5 now everyone."

The director yelled from across the room. The set was bigger than before and we were on course for wrapping up season 3. Natasha was addressing the crew again on the possible angles while on her way to the cafeteria downstairs. I reclaimed my favorite spot next to the open window and proceeded to check-in about the plans with everyone on the group chat.

Me : So we are on for this weekend right?

Rina: I am legit 40,000 feet above the ground texting you. What more do you want?

Sana: Kiaraaaa! See she is flexin again!

Rina: Hey! I am not. I am just saying that I am so serious about being with you for your birthday weekend that I am already on a flight to you. Now appreciate me!

Sana: ugh! I can't with this woman. See you all soon.

I chuckled at the exchange and proceeded to check the script for the next author schedule. I couldn't help but beam with joy reading the bold letters in black - Raul Rathan.

The last one year has been a momentous one for all - John finally began his new venture with Dad and it seemed to be slowly but gradually picking up; Natasha has been busier than ever working on season 3 of my show which was now bigger in comparison with more screen time, solid viewership, good sponsors and bigger sets may I add; Sana got married and her company merged with an international firm which led her to handle high profile clients; Rina got engaged with Jake and permanently moved to Paris to take care of her restaurant, Leaving cute little Muffy under my care permanently. ; And Raul opened his bookstore cafe a few months back.

Our book 'Relentless' that we had worked on together became a hit in the bestseller section and went on to gain more attention than we expected. So much so that I was offered another book deal but I turned it down to follow my actual passion instead - broadcasting and production. And Raul finally moved on from the title of "ghostwriter" to an "author".

I smiled unconsciously as I rubbed my fingers across his name on the page.

"Hey sweetheart! What are you looking at?" Raul said, slightly kissing my forehead. He looked extremely handsome in a grey plaid suit and seemed to be the point of focus of the entire room. The man was just in time for his part of the interview segment.

"Nothing! Just you!", I said flirtatiously to which he chuckled. His pearly whites added to his charm.

A few minutes later Natasha walked over to brief us about our segment. There was a weird tension in the room as we were coming to a close.

"So Mr.Raul! Anything else you would like to say for our viewers and avid readers?", I asked gleefully with an eagerness to close the show faster and head home with my man.

"Ah! Yes! But actually to you Ms.Sen!"

I was alarmed by the off-script dialogue and turned around to almost yell 'cut' in order to check with Raul but I was surprised and in awe by what he did next. Raul was down on his knees, a beautiful diamond ring in a box was held towards me and the whole set had dropped dead in silence.

"I would like you to keep changing the narrative of my story for the rest of my chapters. Would you make me the happiest by…"

"Yes"

I didn't need time to think this time. I truly was in love with The Boy Who Wrote My Story.